MW00830154

A NARRATIVE OF THE CAPTIVITY OF MRS. JOHNSON

Together With

A NARRATIVE OF JAMES JOHNSON

Indian Captive of Charlestown, NH – 1757

Including

Illustrations of

Mr. and Mrs. John Hastings, Jr. and the "Indian Stones"

A HERITAGE CLASSIC

HERITAGE BOOKS
AN IMPRINT OF HERITAGE BOOKS, INC.

Books, CDs, and more—Worldwide

For our listing of thousands of titles see our website
at
www.HeritageBooks.com

Published 1990 by
HERITAGE BOOKS, INC.
Publishing Division
65 East Main Street
Westminster, Maryland 21157-5026

Copyright of new material ©1990 by Barbara M. Jones

All rights reserved. No part of this book may be reproduced or
transmitted in any form or by any means, electronic or mechanical,
including photocopying, recording or by any information storage and
retrieval system without written permission from the author, except for
the inclusion of brief quotations in a review.

International Standard Book Number: 1-55613-337-5

TABLE OF CONTENTS

Illustrations
Mrs. Susanna (Willard) (Johnson) Hastings, Jr.
Mr. Hastings, Jr.
Indian Stones
(Captions by Barbara M. Jones)

Foreword to the New Edition
By Barbara M. Jones

Part 1
A Narrative of the Captivity of Mrs. Johnson

Part 2
Narrative of James Johnson
Indian captive of Charlestown, NH – 1757

iii

MR. and MRS. JOHN HASTINGS, JR.

The portraits of Mr. and Mrs. John Hastings, Jr. are owned by a descendant of Susanna (Willard) (Johnson) Hastings, Jr. The oil on canvas paintings were done by the itinerant painter, William Jennys, after 1800 in Charlestown, New Hampshire. Jennys painted actively from 1793-1807 in the lower and upper Connecticut River Valley. The scar on Mrs. Susanna Hastings, Jr.'s forehead was from an accident when a horse was spooked.

Owned by Kate S. Rowland (Mrs. John Carrere).
Photograph courtesy of Barbara M. Jones (Mrs. Warner E. Jones).

THE ORIGINAL SETTING OF THE "INDIAN STONES"

According to Rev. Henry H. Saunderson's *History of Charlestown, New Hampshire*, Susanna (Willard) (Johnson) Hastings made three trips to the sites of the encampment and birth to locate the exact location. About a half mile from the encampment, Peter Labaree agreed with Mrs. Hastings that the birth took place "on the northeast corner lot of land in Cavendish, about half a mile from the main road leading from Weathersfield to Reading." This is on Knapp Brook Road (Gulf Road). She then engaged a stone cutter to carve the stones and place them on the designated sites but he did not. Both were placed by the main road leading from Weathersfield to Reading, Vermont in 1799. In 1918, Laura Billings Lee, a descendant, had the slabs set into a block of granite for protection. After a number of moves, the stones in 1975 were placed in a mini-park as part of Reading's Bicentennial observance, only a few feet from their original location on Route 106.

The inscription on the larger stone is:

"This is near the spot that the Indians encamped the night after they took Mr. Johnson and family, Mr. Labaree and Farnsworth, August 30, 1754. And Mrs. Johnson was delivered of her child half a mile up this brook.

> When trouble's near the Lord is kind
> He hears the captive cry.
> He can subdue the savage mind
> And learn it sympathy."

The inscription on the smaller stone is:

"On the 31st of August 1754 Capt. James Johnson had a daughter born on this spot of ground being captivated with his whole family by the Indians."

Mrs. Hastings wrote this verse for the smaller birth stone:

> "If mothers e'er should wander here
> They'll drop a sympathetic tear For her, who in the howling wild
> Was safe delivered of a child."

The verse above does not appear, however, on the stone.

Henry Leland Clarke Picture Collection with permission of David Proper, Librarian, Henry N. Flynt Library, Historic Deerfield, Inc. Photograph courtesy of Barbara M. Jones (Mrs. Warner E. Jones).

FOREWORD TO THE NEW EDITION

The Great River, as the Connecticut River was called, flows from the Canadian border to Long Island Sound. The river is the western boundary of New Hampshire and its bank the eastern boundary of Vermont. In the 1600's, the Massachusetts Bay Colony chartered the land along the Great River in the Upper Connecticut River Valley.

Major Simon Willard was prominent in the early life of the Massachusetts Bay Colony and father of seventeen children. Some of his descendants were soldiers at Fort Dummer (now under water at Brattleboro, VT) and land speculators in the Valley.

Above Fort Dummer, to township No. 4, came the Farnsworth brothers in 1740, sons of Samuel and Mary (Whitcomb) (Willard) Farnsworth of Groton. Samuel never married but David and Stephen married Hannah and Eunice Hastings. They were followed by Isaac Parker and Obadiah Sartwell of Groton; Phineas Stevens, grandson of Cyprian and Mary (Willard) Stevens, and son of Deacon Joseph and Prudence (Rice) Stevens of Rutland; John and Hannah (White) Hastings of Hatfield; Moses and Susanna (Hastings) Willard of Lancaster; and others. Hannah, Eunice, and Susanna Hastings were sisters.

In her introduction to Charlestown, Mrs. Johnson tells of the Sunday, June 19, 1746, ambuscade. John Maynard, a soldier, left a detailed plan of No. 4 and the fight. From his plan, the reconstructed Fort at No. 4 was built: antique dealer Leonard P. Goulding discovered the plan and sold it to Horace Brown who shared it with a group of people who raised money to establish the museum; the plan was given upon Brown's death to Yale University. The items recovered after the ambuscade were sold for 40 pounds old tener. In the fight not one man was killed, but four were wounded.

The Three Day Siege at Fort No. 4 was April 7 - 10, 1747. "Mons. Debelcie" was Chevalier Jean Baptiste Boucher de Niverville. He was gone two months with a party of French and Indians that consisted of about sixty men. When they returned to Montreal they brought no prisoners, only a few scalps, but had "committed great deprivations in the enemy's country." The Fort has published a booklet on the siege.

When the boundary dispute between the Massachusetts Bay Colony and New Hampshire was settled Gov. Benning Wentworth of New Hampshire not only chartered the towns in the western part of the state but also in Vermont. In 1753 No. 4 was chartered as Charlestown.

The summer of 1754 marked the beginning of the French and Indian War known in Europe as the Seven Year's War. It was the custom of the French to encourage the Indians to make raids on the English colonies. By taking captives, the French made their enemy help pay the expense of war by paying ransom. The French and Indians both benefited at the expense of the English.

ix

A true pioneer woman, Susanna (Willard) (Johnson) Hastings, the daughter of Moses and Susanna Willard, left a remarkable record of life in the wilderness at Charlestown. She married twice, firstly Capt. James Johnson and secondly John Hastings, Jr., and had fourteen children, five of whom died in infancy. In an Indian raid, the Johnson family, Miriam Willard, Peter Labaree, and Ebenezer Farnsworth were taken from the cabin on the east side of the north end of Main Street. A DAR marker on the lawn is testimony that the cabin still stands although it is masked by many renovations. From here they began their ordeal in captivity. On the second day of her captivity, Mrs. Johnson gave birth to Elizabeth Captive Johnson. (In later years, Mrs. Johnson had two slate slabs carved, the larger describes the capture and the smaller commemorates the birth.) According to State Papers, the Abenaki Indians of St. Francis came to No. 4 that day "because the English had set down upon lands there which they had not purchased."

While in Canada, Mrs. Johnson met "Captains Strowbrow and Vambram" who gave her money at Montreal and food at Quebec. Major Robert Stobo and Capt. Jacob VanBraam had surrendered to the French as part of the capitulation of Fort Necessity. Stobo's story is told in *The Most Extraordinary Adventures of Major Roberts Stobo* by Robert C. Alberts.

James Johnson's deposition of November 14, 1757 has been included with notes by George Waldo Browne. Upon his return from captivity, Capt. James Johnson went to Ticonderoga. Sergeant Thomas Putnam of Charlestown was in his company and witnessed his instant death. Putnam is quoted in Saunderson's *History of Charlestown, New Hampshire*, "His body was left on the ground, but his arms and equipage, together with some of his clothing were brought off. I was acquainted with him from my youth – knew him in the former war when a Lieutenant under the command of Edward Hartwell, Esq., posted at Lunenburg, Townsend, and Narragansett, No.2, etc. He was universally beloved by his company and equally lamented at his death. He was the soldiers friend and a friend to his country – was of easy manners, pleasant, good humored, yet strict to obey his orders and see that those under his command did the same."

Capt. James Johnson's widow returned to Charlestown in 1759. Her husband's estate had to be settled. John Hastings, Jr. and William Heywood appraised real estate Ł219.10.0 sterling, personal estate Ł 96.0.5 sterling, receipts Ł229.16.7 3/4 sterling and expenditures Ł 573.19.5 1/2 sterling. She immediately opened a small store and from 1760-1 held a license required of "Innholders, Taverners and Common Victualers." She probably sold spirits and possibly took in boarders. In 1762 she married John Hastings, Jr.

In 1796 the first edition of her book appeared. The Hon. John C. Chamberlain, a Charlestown lawyer, and contributor of articles to *Farmer's Weekly Museum*, a notable paper at that time in the State, wrote the narrative. The paper and book were published in Walpole, NH, by Isaiah Thomas and David Carlisle who owned the printshop and bookstore. The second edition, 1807, was printed in Windsor, VT, by Alden Spooner and the third edition with notes and appendix, 1814, was printed in Windsor, VT, by Thomas Pomeroy. Both the second and third editions were revised and edited by Mrs. (Johnson) Hastings.

She had been working on the third edition before her death on November 27, 1810 at Langdon, NH. John Hastings, Jr. had died in 1804 and she was in her eighties. There are errors in the book. Her memory for facts had apparently become impaired. Many editions have appeared since then in this country and England.

In Forest Hill Cemetery, East Street, stands a monument erected by the descendants of the captives on August 30, 1870. The shaft stands in the Briggs Hill Road side of the cemetery, not far from the graves of Susanna and John Hastings, Jr. At the nonprofit museum, The Fort at No. 4, on Route 11 approximately one mile from the site of the original fort on Main Street, is displayed the door from the Johnson cabin. Traces of the red earth and milk paint, old hinges of strap iron, latch and string closure and hatchet marks are a reminder of that day in 1754.

Barbara M. Jones (Mrs. Warner E.), B.S., M.S.
Historian, Old Fort No. 4 Associates
April 15, 1990

Indian Captivities Series

THE CAPTIVITY
OF
MRS. JOHNSON

A
NARRATIVE
OF THE
CAPTIVITY
OF

Mrs. JOHNSON.

CONTAINING

An ACCOUNT of her SUFFERINGS,
during *Four Years* with the INDIAN
and FRENCH.

Published according to Act of Congress.

PRINTED AT WALPOLE, NEWHAMP.
BY DAVID CARLISLE.
1796.

A

NARRATIVE

OF THE

CAPTIVITY OF MRS. JOHNSON

REPRINTED FROM THE THIRD EDITION, PUBLISHED
AT WINDSOR, VERMONT, 1814
WITH ALL CORRECTIONS AND ADDITIONS

THE H. R. HUNTTING COMPANY
SPRINGFIELD, MASSACHUSETTS
MCMVII

IV

- Notice -

The foxing, or discoloration with age, characteristic of
old books, sometimes shows through to some extent in
reprints such as this, especially when the foxing is
very severe in the original book. We feel that the
contents of this book warrant its reissue despite these
blemishes, and hope you will agree and read it with
pleasure.

*This edition is limited to 350 numbered copies,
of which the first 50 copies (Nos. I to 50) are
on Van Gelder handmade paper, and the remaining 300 copies (Nos. 51 to 350) are on Alex-
andria all-rag paper.*

This volume is No............................

Facsimile Reprint

Published 1990 By
HERITAGE BOOKS, INC.
1540 Pointer Ridge Place, Bowie, Maryland 20716
(301)-390-7709

ISBN 1-55613-337-5

DISTRICT OF VERMONT, TO WIT:

BE it remembered, that on the thirteenth day of April, in the thirty eighth year of the Independence of the United States of America, ELIZABETH CAPTIVE KIMBALL, of the said district, hath deposited in this office the title of a book, the right whereof she claims as proprietor, in the words following to wit:

L. S.

"*A Narrative of the Captivity of Mrs. Johnson. Containing an account of her sufferings during four years with the Indians and French. Together with an appendix, containing the Sermons preached at her funeral, and that of her mother, with sundry other interesting articles. Third edition, corrected and considerably enlarged.*"

In conformity to the act of the Congress of the United States, entitled "An Act for the encouragement of learning, by securing the copies of maps, charts and books to the authors and proprietors of such copies during the times therein mentioned."

JESSE GOVE,
Clerk of the District of Vermont.

A true Copy of Record,
Examined and Sealed by J. GOVE, *Clerk.*

PUBLISHERS' ANNOUNCEMENT

The Captivity of Mrs. Johnson is the first of a series of reprints of histories of Indian Captivities which will comprise the more important of these works dealing with a picturesque and important phase of early Colonial history. These narratives not only give a clear view of many of the habits and customs of the American Indians and of the dangers and hardships of Colonial life, but are, as well, fascinating simply as stories.

Copies of most of these books have become scarce, and are only to be found in a few large libraries, or here and there among private owners. The publishers are assured that these reprints will meet a real demand.

The books of the series will be carefully edited with introductions and notes. They will be uniform in style, type, paper, and binding, and no pains will be spared to make them accurate and artistic reproductions of the best editions of the originals.

For assistance in the preparation of the present volume of the series, the publishers desire to acknowledge their indebtedness to Horace W. Bailey, Esq., who has furnished the historical introduction, to Wilberforce Eames, Esq., who has furnished much valuable data in relation to the early editions of the work, and to Thomas W. Peck, Librarian, Walpole, N. H., for the loan of the first edition.

BIBLIOGRAPHY

A ‖ NARRATIVE ‖ OF THE ‖ CAPTIVITY ‖ OF ‖ MRS. JOHNSON. ‖ CONTAINING ‖ AN ACCOUNT OF HER SUFFERINGS, ‖ DURING FOUR YEARS WITH THE INDIANS ‖ AND FRENCH. ‖ PUBLISHED ACCORDING TO ACT OF CONGRESS. ‖ PRINTED AT WALPOLE, NEWHAMPSHIRE, ‖ BY DAVID CARLISLE, JUN. ‖ 1796. ‖ 12 mo, pp. 144.

A ‖ NARRATIVE ‖ OF THE ‖ CAPTIVITY ‖ OF ‖ MRS. JOHNSON. ‖ CONTAINING ‖ AN ACCOUNT OF HER SUFFERINGS, ‖ DURING FOUR YEARS, WITH THE INDIANS ‖ AND FRENCH. ‖ PUBLISHED ACCORDING TO ACT OF CONGRESS. ‖ SECOND EDITION, CORRECTED AND ENLARGED. ‖ WINDSOR, (VT.) ‖ PRINTED BY ALDEN SPOONER. ‖ 1807. ‖ 18 mo, pp. 144.

A ‖ NARRATIVE ‖ OF THE ‖ CAPTIVITY OF MRS. JOHNSON. ‖ CONTAINING ‖ AN ACCOUNT OF HER SUFFERINGS, DURING ‖ FOUR YEARS, WITH THE IN- ‖ DIANS AND FRENCH. ‖ TOGETHER WITH AN ‖ APPENDIX: ‖ CONTAINING THE SERMONS, PREACHED AT HER FUNERAL, AND THAT OF ‖ HER MOTHER; WITH SUNDRY OTHER INTERESTING ARTICLES. ‖ THIRD EDITION CORRECTED, AND CONSIDERABLY ENLARGED. ‖ WINDSOR, (VT.) ‖ PRINTED BY THOMAS M. POMROY. ‖ 1814. ‖ 12 mo, pp. 178.

A ‖ NARRATIVE OF THE CAPTIVITY ‖ OF MRS. JOHNSON. ‖ LOWELL DANIEL BIXBY 1834. ‖ 18 mo, pp. 150.

A ‖ NARRATIVE ‖ OF THE ‖ CAPTIVITY ‖ OF ‖ MRS. JOHNSON, ‖ CONTAINING ‖ AN ACCOUNT OF HER SUFFERINGS, DURING ‖ FOUR YEARS, WITH THE INDIANS ‖ AND FRENCH. ‖ New York: ‖ 1841. ‖ 18 mo, pp. 111.
*No indication of printer or publisher.

NARRATIVE OF THE CAPTIVITY OF MRS. JOHNSON, OF CHARLESTOWN, N. H. CONTAINING AN ACCOUNT OF HER SUFFERINGS, DURING FOUR YEARS WITH THE

INDIANS AND FRENCH. (In Farmer and Moore's Collections, Topographical, Historical, and Biographical, relating principally to New-Hampshire, Vol. 1, pp. 177-239. Concord: published by Hill and Moore, 1822.) Also, Concord: reprinted by H. E. and J. W. Moore, 1831.

HISTORICAL ADDRESS ‖ AT THE ‖ DEDICATION OF A MONUMENT ‖ IN ‖ CHARLESTOWN, N. H. ‖ BY REV. B. LABAREE, D.D., LL.D. ‖ LATE PRESIDENT OF MIDDLEBURY COLLEGE, VERMONT. ‖ BOSTON: ‖ PRESS OF T. R. MARVIN & SON, 131 CONGRESS STREET. ‖ 1870. ‖ 8 vo, pp. 28.

There were also two English editions in pamphlet form: Newcastle; M. Augus, 1797. 18 mo, pp. 72; and an edition published by J. and P. Wilson, 1802. 12 mo, pp. 24.

INTRODUCTION

A word in regard to the settlements in the Connecticut Valley antedating the time of the opening of the narrative of the captivity of Mrs. Johnson will clear the way for a better understanding of the story.

The upper Connecticut Valley and the State of Vermont were never the permanent abiding place of an Indian tribe. Indian families often found the rich unwooded interval lands in the valley convenient and comfortable squatting places for a season or two at a time, and at such times the soil was cultivated, chiefly for the growing of corn. The valley of the Connecticut River and the Lake Champlain Valley, or rather the river and the lake themselves, were Indian highways for two centuries, beginning with the advent of the French into Canada under the master hand of Samuel de Champlain, during the opening years of the seventeenth century. The history of these two great highways of the early days bristles with accounts of bloody attacks and counter attacks made by the French and Algonquins on the north, the English and Iroquois on the south. The story of the wanton cruelties of these attacks, of the burning and pillaging of homes, the capture and often the savage murder of helpless women and innocent children, makes a tale of horrors too revolting, too inhuman, to be included in the annals of civilized warfare. By the close of 1636, settlements were well under way at Wethersfield, Windsor, Hartford, and Springfield, in the lower valley, with a total population of about one thousand. Then followed the stern, rugged push of settlement up both sides of the river in Massachusetts. A forge ahead into the wilds, then a surging back to the more populous and better fortified settlements, was the procedure for many years. The French Crown granted seigniories, and the English Crown charters, with profligacy, but the story of taking, holding, and keeping the land was written in blood.

Up to 1723, Northfield in Massachusetts, which included what is now Hinsdale in New Hampshire and Vernon in Vermont (all then supposed to be within the jurisdiction of Massachusetts), was the outpost of civilization in the valley. Fort Dummer, now Brattleboro, became the outpost in 1724. The site of the Old Fort is now marked by a granite monument which is situated a mile south of the Brattleboro station, and about 50 rods easterly from, and within plain sight of, the railroad. Fort Dummer, with the settlement gathered about it, held the honor of outpost until 1740. Here was the birthplace of Colonel John Sargent, the first white person born in Vermont (1732). In 1740, a few families struggled on up the river to Charlestown, New Hampshire (No. 4), and old No. 4 held the outpost honor until the settlement, in 1762, of Newbury, Vermont, and Haverhill, New Hampshire, in the Coos Country, sixty miles up the river. The story of Charlestown, with its fort and its handful of brave soldiers and settlers, during the early years leading up to the opening chapter of our story, is a counterpart of that of the beginnings of the towns to the south. At the opening of the narrative, in 1754, Charlestown had been for fourteen years a military post, and the most northerly white settlement, subject, of course, to the rule of alternate occupancy and vacating. The site of the Old Fort at Charlestown is marked by a suitable monument, erected and dedicated by the co-operation of the Union historical societies of Charlestown, New Hampshire, and Springfield, Vermont, on August 30, 1904, the one hundred and fiftieth anniversary of the raid on the fort and of the captivity of Mrs. Johnson.

These stories of Indian raids are historical gems, especially when the persons taken captive were moved to chronicle their experiences in enduring type. The writers were not in the commercial lists, but for the most part seem to have been actuated by a spirit of thankfulness and gratitude to Almighty God for remarkable deliverances, their narratives being characterized throughout by good old Puritanic piety. The Johnson narrative is no exception to the general rule, and has but little in its subject matter that does not bear directly and concisely upon the beginnings and making of our New England homes. Written by a mother who gave birth to a promising daughter under such peculiar and trying circumstances, it is not strange that great emphasis should be given to this event. The narrative gives an unclouded view of the conditions surrounding a military post and a new settlement on the extreme frontier. It uncovers the Indian trail into Canada, discloses aboriginal habits and mode of life and warfare, and gives an insight into the captivities of the great New France of that era. The reader of these narratives does not need to be a master of logic to discover that the founders of our homes were refined, intelligent, very religiously inclined, and physically robust.

The reader will be interested in Mrs. Johnson's story of the locating, nearly fifty years after the event, of the spot where her daughter was born. The stones, a cut of which is reproduced in this volume (by the courtesy of The Tuttle Company, of Rutland, Vermont, publishers of *Conant's History of Vermont*) stand in the town of Reading, Vermont, but the daughter was born "a half mile up the brook," in the town of Cavendish. The *History of Charlestown, New Hampshire*, says in substance that Mrs. Johnson negotiated for these monuments, prepared the inscriptions, and directed that the smaller stone should be placed upon the spot where her child was born, while the larger should mark the place where the Indians encamped; but regardless of her instructions the stones were placed together on the main road leading from Wethersfield to Reading—and here they have stood for a century.

Elizabeth Captive Johnson, the third white person born in Vermont, lived to womanhood, and became the wife of Colonel George Kimball. One of her daughters married Jason Wetherby, and her daughter married Oel Billings, the father of the late Frederick Billings of Woodstock, Vermont, one of the most distinguished sons of the Green Mountain State.

The book itself, *The Captivity of Mrs. Johnson*, is one of the rarest Vermont productions. The story was first told by John C. Chamberlain, and published at Walpole, N. H., in 1796. The second edition was printed at Windsor, Vermont, in 1807. The third edition, enlarged with notes and appendix (the edition now reproduced), was printed at Windsor, in 1814. The last two editions are largely Mrs. Johnson's own handiwork, and were revised and edited at her request. She died November 27, 1810, at the age of 81 years, a month or two after finishing the manuscript of the last edition of her book.

HORACE W. BAILEY.

Newbury, Vt., July, 1907.

A

NARRATIVE

OF THE

CAPTIVITY

OF

Mrs. JOHNSON.

———◆———

INTRODUCTION.

NOTICES OF THE WILLARD FAMILY.

TO trace the progress of families, from their origin to the present day, when perhaps they are spread over the four quarters of the globe, and no memorandums are found except in the uncertain pages of memory, is a task which can be but feebly performed. In noticing the name of Willard, which was my family name, I cannot pretend to accuracy; but the information which I have collected will perhaps be of some service to others, who possess a greater stock; and if the various branches of families would contribute their mites, it would be an easy way of remedying the deficiency, which at present exists in American genealogy.

The first person by the name of Willard who settled in this country, was Major Willard, whose name is recorded in the history of New-England wars. In the year sixteen hundred and seventy five, in the time of "Philip's war," a notorious Indian who lived within the present limits of the state of Rhode Island, Major Willard who then lived in the town of Lancaster in Massachusetts, commanded a troop of horse; and among his vigorous services, he relieved the town of Brookfield from the Nipnet Indians, who had burnt every house but one, and had almost reduced that to capitulation. When Lancaster was destroyed by the Indians, Major Willard removed to Salem, where he spent the rest of his days. He had two sons, one of whom was a settled minister in the town of Groton; which place he was driven from by the Indians, and was afterwards installed in Boston. His other son, Simon, established himself on Still River, since taken from Lancaster, and incorporated into the town of Harvard. He had nine sons, Simon, Henry, Hezekiah, John, Joseph, Josiah, Samuel, Jonathan and James; Josiah removed to Winchester in New-Hampshire, and afterwards commanded Fort Dummer; the rest inherited the substance of their father, and lived to very advanced ages in the vicinity of their birth.—They all left numerous families, who spread over the United States. His eldest son, Simon, was my grandfather; he had two sons, Aaron and Moses: Aaron lived in Lancaster, and Moses, my father, removed to Lunenburg. I ought to remark, that my grandmother Willard, after the death of her husband, married a person by the name of Farnsworth, by whom she had three sons, who were the first settlers of Charlestown, No. 4—one of them was killed by the Indians.

My father had twelve children; he removed to Charlestown, No. 4, in 1742, and soon had the pleasure to find his children settled around him: he was killed by the Indians in 1756.—My mother died in May, 1797,* and had lived to see twelve children, ninety-two grandchildren, one hundred and twenty-three great grand-children, and four great-great-grand-children. The whole that survive are now settled on Connecticut River.

NOTICES OF MR. JAMES JOHNSON.

IN the year 1730, my great-uncle, Colonel Josiah Willard, while at Boston, was invited

---

*At the age of eighty-four, she busied herself in making a coverlid, which contains something of the remarkable—she did not quite complete it, it now contains upwards of five thousand pieces.

to take a walk on the long-wharf, to view some transports who had just landed from Ireland; a number of gentlemen present were viewing the exercise of some lads who were placed on shore, to exhibit their activity to those who wished to purchase. My uncle spied a boy of some vivacity, of about ten years of age, and who was the only one in the crew who spoke English: he bargained for him. I have never been able to learn the price; but as he was afterwards my husband, I am willing to suppose it a considerable sum. He questioned the boy respecting his parentage and descent. All the information he could get was, that young James, a considerable time previous, went to sea with his uncle, who commanded a ship and had the appearance of a man of property, that this uncle was taken sick at sea and died; immediately after his death they came in sight of this ship of Irish transports, and he was put on board. His being the only one of the crew who spoke English, and other circumstances, have led his friends to conclude that this removal on board the Irish ship, was done to facilitate the sequestration of his uncle's property. He lived with Col. Willard until he was twenty years old, and then bought the other year of his time. In 1748 Gov. Shirley gave him a lieutenant's commission under Edward Hartwell, Esq.

SITUATION OF THE COUNTRY IN 1744.

It is an old maxim, that after a man is in possession of a small independent property, it is easy for him to acquire a great fortune; just so with countries;—possess them of a few inhabitants, and let those be unmolested by Indians and enemies, the land will soon swarm with inhabitants. But when a feeble band only are gathered together, and obliged to contend with pestilence, famine and the sword, their melancholy numbers will decrease and waste away. The situation of our ancestors has often been described in language that did honor to the hearts that conceived it. The boisterous ocean, with unknown shores hemmed them in on one side, and a forest, swarming with savages, yelling for their blood, threatened on the other. But the same undaunted spirit which has defended them in so many perils, buoyed them above despair in their early struggles for safety and liberty. I shall be pardoned for the digression when I observe, that I have in all my travels felt a degree of pride in recollecting, that I belonged to a country whose valor was distinguished, and whose spirit had never been debased by servile submission.

At the age of fourteen, in 1744, I made a visit from Leominster to Charlestown, to visit my parents. Thro' a long wilderness from

Lunenburg to Lower Ashuelot, now Swanzey, we travelled two days; a solitary house was all the mark of cultivation that occurred on the journey. Guided by marked trees, we travelled cautiously through the gloomy forest, where now the well-till'd farms occupy each rod of ground; from Ashuelot to Charlestown the passage was opposed, now by "the hill of difficulty," and now by the slough despond. A few solitary inhabitants, who appeared the representatives of wretchedness, were scattered on the way.

When I approached the town of Charlestown, the first object that met my eyes was a party of Indians holding a war dance, a cask of rum which the inhabitants had suffered them to partake of, had raised their spirits to all the horrid yells, and feats of distortion which characterize the nation. I was chilled at the sight and passed tremblingly by. At this time Charlestown contained nine or ten families, who lived in huts not far distant from each other. The Indians were numerous, and associated in a friendly manner with the whites. It was the most northerly settlement on Connecticut River, and the adjacent country was terribly wild. A sawmill was erected, and the first boards were sawed while I was there: the inhabitants commemorated the event with a dance, which took place on the new boards. In those days there was such a mixture on the frontiers, of savages and settlers, without established laws to govern them, that the state of society cannot be easily described, and the impending dangers of war, where it was known that the savages would join the enemies of our country, retarded the progress of refinement and cultivation. The inhabitants of Charlestown began to erect a fort, and took some steps towards clearing their farms; but war soon checked their industry.

CHARLESTOWN.

IN the year 1740, the first settlement was made in the town of Charlestown, then known by the name of No. 4, by three families who emigrated from Lunenburg, by the name of Farnsworth; that part of New-Hampshire west of Merrimac River was then a trackless wilderness. Within a few years past instances have been known, of new townships totally uninhabited, becoming thick settled villages in the course of six or seven years. But in those days, when government was weak, when savages were on our borders and Frenchmen in Canada, population extended with timorous and tardy paces; in the course of twelve years the families increased only to twenty two or three. The human race will not flourish unless fostered by the warm sunshine of peace.

During the first twenty years of its existence as a settled place, until the peace between Great-Britain and France, it suffered all the consternation and ravages of war; not that warfare which civilized nations wage with each other, but the cruel carnage of savages and Frenchmen. Sometimes engaged in the duties of the camp, at others sequestering themselves from surrounding enemies, they became familiar with danger, but not with industrious husbandry.

In the year 1744, the inhabitants began to erect a fort for their safety. When the Cape Breton war commenced, the Indians assumed the hatchet and began their depredations on Charlestown on the 19th day of April, A. D. 1746, by burning the mills and taking Captain John Spafford, Isaac Parker, and Stephen Farnsworth prisoners. On the second of May following Seth Putnam was killed. Two days after Capt. Payne arrived with a troop of horse from Massachusetts, to defend the place;—about twenty of his men had the curiosity to view the place where Putnam was killed, and were ambushed by the Indians. Capt. Stevens, who commanded a few men rushed out of the fort to their relief; a sharp combat ensued, in which the Indians were routed: they left some guns and blankets on the field of action, but they carried their dead off with them, which is a policy they never omit. Ensign

Obadiah Sartwell was captured, and Samuel Farnsworth, Elijah Allen, Peter Perin, Aaron Lyon and Joseph Massey fell victims to Indian vengeance.

On the 19th of June a severe engagement took place. Capt. Brown, from Stow in Massachusetts, had previously arrived with some troops; a party of his, joined a number of Capt. Stevens' soldiers to go into the meadow after their horses. The dogs discovered an ambush, which put them into a posture for action, and gave them the advantage of the first fire. This disconcerted the savages, who being on higher ground over-shot, and did but little damage to the English. The enemy were routed, and even seen to drag several dead bodies after them. They left behind them guns, spears, and blankets, which sold at 40l. old tenor. During the time Capt. Josiah Brown assisted in defending the fort, Jedediah Winchel was killed, Samuel Stanhope, Coronet Baker and David Parker were wounded. During this summer the fort was entirely blockaded, and all were obliged to take refuge within the piquets. On the 3d day of August one Phillips was killed within a few feet of the fort, as he accidentally stepped out; at night a soldier crept to him with a rope, and he was drawn into the fort and interred. In the summer of the year 1746, Capt. Ephraim Brown from Sudbury,

arrived with a troop of horse to relieve Capt.
Josiah Brown. The Sudbury troop tarried
about a month, and were relieved by a company commanded by Capt. Winchester, who
defended the place till autumn, when the inhabitants, fatigued with watching, and weary
of the dangers of the forest, deserted the
place entirely for about six months. In the
month of August previous to the evacuation,
the Indians assisted by their brethren the
French, were very troublesome and mischievous; they destroyed all the horses, hogs
and cattle. An attack was made on the fort,
which lasted two days. My father at this
time lost ten cattle, but the people were
secured behind their wooden walls, and received but little damage.

In this recess of the settlement of No. 4, the
Indians and French were ice-locked in Canada, and the frontiers suffered only in apprehension. In March 1747, Capt. Phinehas
Stevens, who commanded a ranging party of
about 30 men, marched to No. 4, and took
possession of the fort. He found it uninjured
by the enemy, and an old spaniel and a cat,
who had been domesticated before the evacuation, had guarded it safely thro' the winter,
and gave the troops a hearty welcome to their
tenement.

Capt. Stevens was of eminent service to the
infant settlement. In 1748 he moved his

family to the place, and encouraged the settlers by his fortitude and industry. In the
early part of his life, when Rutland suffered
by savage vengeance, when the Rev. Mr. Willard was murdered, he was taken prisoner and
carried to St. Francis. This informed him of
the Indian customs, and familiarized him
with their mode of warfare: he was an active,
penetrating soldier, and a respectable, worthy
citizen.

In a few days after the fort was taken possession of by Capt. Stevens's troops, a party of
500 French and Indians, commanded by
Mons. Debelcie, sallied from their den in
Canada, and made a furious attack on the
fort. The battle lasted five days, and every
stratagem which French policy or Indian
malice could invent, was practised to reduce
the garrison. Sometimes they made an onset
by a discharge of musquetry, at others they
discharged fire arrows, which communicated
fire to several parts of the fort. But these
were insufficient to daunt the courage of the
little band that were assailed. Their next
step was to fill a cart with combustibles, and
roll it against the walls, to communicate fire;
but the English kept up such a brisk incessant
fire that they were defeated in the project.
At length the Monsieurs, tired with fighting,
beat a parley; two Indians, formerly acquainted with Capt. Stevens, came as negoci-

ators, and wished to exchange some furs for corn; this Capt. Stevens refused, but offered a bushel of corn for each hostage they would leave to be exchanged, at some future day. These terms were not complied with, and on the fifth day the enemy retreated, at which time the soldiers in the garrison honored them with as brisk a discharge as they could afford, to let them know that they were neither disheartened nor exhausted in ammunition. The garrison had none killed, and only one, by the name of Brown, was wounded.

Perhaps no place was ever defended with greater bravery than this fort during this action; 30 or 40 men, when attacked by 500, must have an uncommon degree of fortitude and vigilance to defend themselves during a siege of five days. But Capt. Stevens was equal to the task, and will be applauded by posterity. After the battle he sent an express to Boston with the tidings. Gov. Charles Knowles happened to be then at Boston, and rewarded Capt. Stevens with a handsome sword, in gratitude for which the place was afterwards called *Charlestown*.

In November 1747, a body of the troops set out from the fort, to return to Massachusetts: they had not proceeded far before the Indians fired on them. Isaac Goodale and Nathaniel Gould were killed, and one Ander-

son taken prisoner. From this period until
the end of the Cape Breton war, the fort was
defended by Capt. Stevens. Soldiers passed
and repassed to Canada, but the inhabitants
took sanctuary in the fort, and made but little
progress in cultivation. During the Indian
wars, which lasted till the year 1760, Charlestown was noted more for its feats of war, than
a place of rapid improvement. Settlers thought
it more prudent to remain with their friends in
safety, than risk their scalps with savage
power. Since that period, it has become a
flourishing village, and contains all that a
rural situation affords of the useful and the
pleasant; numerous farms and stately buildings now flourish where the savage roamed
the forest.—The prosperity of the town was
greatly promoted by the Rev. Bulkely Olcott,
who was a settled minister there about 32
years. In the character of this good man was
combined the agreeable companion, the industrious citizen, and unaffected christian. During the whole of his ministry, his solicitude
for the happiness of his parishoners was as
conspicuous, in the benefits they received
from his assistance, as in their sincere attach-
ment to his person. As a divine he was
pathetic, devout and instructive, and may
with propriety be said to have

Shewn the path to heaven, and led the way.

He was highly respected through life: in June, 1793, he died, much lamented.

REMOVAL TO CHARLESTOWN, &c.

IN May 1749, we received information of the cessation of arms between Great Britain and France. I had then been married about two years, and Mr. Johnson's enterprising spirit was zealous to remove to Charlestown; in June we undertook the hazardous and fatiguing journey: we arrived safe at the fort, and found five families, who had ventured so far into the woods during hostilities. But the gloomy forest, and the warlike appearance of the place, soon made me homesick. Two or three days after my arrival, orders came from Massachusetts to withdraw the troops: government placed confidence in the proffered peace of Frenchmen, and withdrew even the appearance of hostility. But French treachery and savage malice will ever keep pace with each other. Without even the suspicion of danger, the inhabitants went about their business of husbandry. The day the soldiers left the fort, Ensign Obadiah Sartwell went to harrow some corn, and took Enos Stevens, the fourth son of Phinehas Stevens, Esq. to ride horse; my father and two brothers were at work in the meadow; early in the afternoon the Indians appeared and shot Ensign Sartwell and the horse, and took young Stevens a prisoner. In addition to this, my father and brothers were in the meadow, and we supposed they must be destroyed.— My husband was gone to Northfield. In the fort were seven women and four men: the anxiety and grief we experienced was the highest imaginable. The next night we dispatched a post to Boston, to carry the news of our disaster, but my father and brothers did not return. The next day but one my husband and five or six others arrived from Northfield. We kept close in the garrison, suffering every apprehension for ten or twelve days, when the sentry from the box cried out that troops were coming: joyful at the relief, we all mounted on the top of the fort, and among the rest discovered my father. He, on hearing the guns, supposed the fort was destroyed, left his team in the meadow, and made the best of his way to Northfield with my two brothers.—The soldiers were about thirty in number, and headed by Major Josiah Willard, of Fort Dummer. Enos Stevens was carried to Montreal, but the French commander sent him back directly, by the way of Albany. This was the last damage done the frontiers during the Cape Breton War.

CURSORY NOTICES.

A detail of the miseries of a "frontier man," must excite the pity of every child of humanity. The gloominess of the rude forest, the distance from friends and competent defence, and the daily inroads and nocturnal yells of hostile Indians, awaken those keen apprehensions and anxieties which conception can only picture. If the peaceful employment of husbandry is pursued, the loaded musket must stand by his side; if he visits a neighbor, or resorts on Sundays to the sacred house of prayer, the weapons of war must bear him company; at home, the distresses of a wife, and the tears of lisping children often unman the soul that real danger assailed in vain. Those who can recollect the war that existed between France and England fifty years ago, may figure to themselves the unhappy situation of the inhabitants on the frontiers of New-Hampshire; the malice of the French in Canada, and the exasperated savages that dwelt in their vicinity, rendered the tedious days and frightful nights a season of unequalled calamities. The daily reports of captured families and slaughtered friends, mingled grief with fear. Had there been an organized government to stretch forth its protecting arm, in any case of danger, the misery might have been in a degree alleviated.

But the infancy of our country did not admit of this blessing. While Governor Shirley of Massachusetts, was petitioning to England for a fleet and army, Benning Wentworth, the governor of New-Hampshire, implicitly obeying the advice of his friend Shirley, remained inactively secure at his seat at Portsmouth. At the commencement of the year 1745, the expedition to Louisburg was projected, the success of which originated from the merest accident, rather than from military valor or generalship; this drained New-Hampshire of most of its effective men. From that period till the peace, which took place in the year 1749, the savages committed frequent depredations on the defenceless inhabitants, and the ease with which they gained their prey, encouraged their boldness, and by scattering in small parties, they were able to infest the whole frontier of New-Hampshire, from fort Dummer on Connecticut river, to the lowest settlement on Merrimack. During this war, which is known by the name of the Cape Breton war, the town of No. 4 could hardly be said to be inhabited; some adventurers had made a beginning, but few were considered as belonging to the town. Capt. Stevens, whose valour is recorded as an instance of consummate generalship, part of the time kept the fort, which afforded a shelter to the enterprising settlers in times of imminent danger.

But even his vigilance did not save the town from numerous scenes of carnage.—At the commencement of the peace, in 1749, the enterprising spirit of New-England rose superior to the dangers of the forest, and they began to venture innovation. The Indians, still thirsty for plunder and rapine, and regardless of the peace which their masters, the French, had concluded, kept up a flying warfare, and committed several outrages upon lives and property; this kept the increasing inhabitants in a state of alarm, for three or four years; most of the time they performed their daily work without molestation, but retreated to the fort at each returning night.

Our country has so long been exposed to Indian wars, that recitals of exploits and sufferings, of escapes and deliverances have become both numerous and trite.—The air of novelty will not be attempted in the following pages; simple facts, unadorned, is what the reader must expect; pity for my sufferings, and admiration at my safe return, is all that my history can excite. The aged man, while perusing, will probably turn his attention to the period when the facts took place, his memory will be refreshed with the sad tidings of his country's sufferings, which gave a daily wound to his feelings, between the years 1740 and 1760; by contrasting those days with the present, he may rejoice that he witnesses those times which many have "waited for, but died without a sight." Those "in early life," while they commisserate the sufferings which their parents and ancestors endured, may felicitate themselves that their lines fell in a land of peace, where neither savages nor neighboring wars molest their happiness.

CHAP. I.

SITUATION UNTIL AUGUST 31, 1754.

SOME of the soldiers who arrived with Major Willard, with the inhabitants who bore arms, were commanded by Capt. Stevens the rest of the year 1749, and part of the following spring; after which the inhabitants resided pretty much in the fort, until the spring or fall of the year 1752. They cultivated their lands in some degree, but they put but little confidence in the savages.

The continuation of peace began by degrees to appease the resentment of the Indians, and they appeared to discover a wish for friendly intercourse. The inhabitants in No. 4, and its vicinity, relaxed their watchfulness, and ventured more boldly into the fields. Every appearance of hostility at length vanished— the Indians expressed a wish to traffic, the inhabitants laid by their fears, and thought no more of tomahawks, nor scalping knives. Mr. Johnson now thought himself justified in removing to his farm, an hundred rods distant from the fort, which was then the uppermost settlement on Connecticut River, he pursued his occupation of trade, and the Indians made frequent visits to traffic their furs for his merchandize. He frequently

credited them for blankets and other necessaries, and in most instances they were punc-
tual in payment. During the year 1753, all
was harmony and safety—settlements increased with tolerable rapidity, and the new
country began to assume the appearance of
cultivation.

The commencement of the year 1754 began
to threaten another rupture between the
French and English, and as the dividing line
between Canada and the English Colonies
was the object of contention, it was readily
seen that the frontier towns would be in imminent danger. But as immediate war was
not expected, Mr. Johnson thought that he
might risk the safety of his family, while he
made a tour to Connecticut, for trade. He
sat out the last of May, and his absence of
three months was a tedious and a bitter
season to me. Soon after his departure every
body was "tremblingly alive" with fear. The
Indians were reported to be on their march
for our destruction, and our distance from
sources of information gave full latitude for
exaggeration of news, before it reached our
ears. The fears of the night were horrible
beyond description, and even the light of day
was far from dispelling painful anxiety.
While looking from the windows of my log-
house, and seeing my neighbors tread cautiously by each hedge and hillock, lest some

secreted savage might start forth to take their scalp, my fears would baffle description. Alarms grew louder and louder, till our apprehensions were too strongly confirmed by the news of the capture of Mr. Malloon's family, on Merrimack River; this reached us about the 20th of August. Imagination now saw and heard a thousand Indians; and I never went round my own house, without first looking with trembling caution by each corner, to see if a tomahawk was not raised for my destruction.

On the 24th of August I was relieved from all my fears by the arrival of my husband.— He brought intelligence from Connecticut that a war was expected the next spring, but that no immediate danger was contemplated. He had made preparations to remove to Northfield, as soon as our stock of hay was consumed, and our dozen of swine had demolished our ample stores of grain, which would secure his family and property from the miseries and ravages of war. Our eldest son, Sylvanus, who was six years old, was in the mean time to be put to school at Springfield. Mr. Johnson brought home a large addition to his stores, and the neighbors made frequent parties at our house, to express their joy for his return, and time passed merrily off, by the aid of spirit and a ripe yard of melons. As I was in the last days of pregnancy, I could not join so heartily in their good cheer as I otherwise might. Yet in a new country, pleasure is often derived from sources unknown to those less accustomed to the woods. The return of my husband, the relief from danger and the crowds of happy friends, combined to render my situation peculiarly agreeable. I now boasted with exultation, that I should, with husband, friends and luxuries, live happy in spite of the fear of savages.

On the evening of the 29th of August our house was visited by a party of neighbors, who spent the time very cheerfully with watermelons and flip, till midnight; they all then retired in high spirits, except a spruce young spark who tarried a few hours longer to keep company with my sister. Unsuspicious of danger we went to bed with feelings well tuned for sleep. But O the transition in the morning! Well would it have been for us if we had observed the caution of the poet.

> " But farewell now to unsuspicious nights,
> And slumbers unalarm'd ! Now ere you sleep
> See that your polish'd arms are prim'd with care,
> And drop the night bolt ;—ruffians are abroad ;
> And the first larum of the cock's shrill throat
> May prove a trumpet, summoning your ear
> To horrid sounds of hostile feet within.
> E'en day-light has its dangers ; and the walk
> Through pathless wastes and woods, unconscious once
> Of other tenants than melodious birds,
> Or harmless flocks, is hazardous and bold."

Beauties of Cowper.

We rested with fine composure, till midway
between daybreak and sunrise, when we were
roused by neighbor Labarree's knocking at
the door, who had shouldered his ax to a day's
work for my husband. Mr. Johnson slipped
on his jacket and trowsers, and stepped to the
door to let him in. But by opening the door
he opened a scene—terrible to describe!! Indians! Indians were the first words I heard,
he sprang to his guns, but Labarree, heedless
of danger, instead of closing the door to keep
them out, began to rally our hired men up
stairs, for not rising earlier. But in an instant
a crowd of savages, fixed horribly for war,
rushed furiously in. I screamed and begged
my friends to ask for quarter; by this time
they were all over the house; some up stairs,
some hauling my sister out of bed, another had
hold of me, and one was approaching Mr.
Johnson, who stood in the middle of the floor
to deliver himself up; but the Indian, supposing that he would make resistance, and be
more than his match, went to the door and
brought three of his comrades, and the four
bound him. I was led to the door, fainting
and trembling; there stood my friend Labarree, bound; Ebenezer Farnsworth, whom
they found up chamber, they were putting in
the same situation, and to complete the shocking scene, my three little children were driven
naked to the place where I stood. On viewing

myself I found that I too was naked. An
Indian had plundered three gowns, who, on
seeing my situation, gave me the whole. I
asked another for a petticoat, but he refused
it. After what little plunder their hurry would
allow them to get, was confusedly bundled up,
we were ordered to march. After going about
20 rods we fell behind a rising ground, where
we halted to pack the things in a better
manner; while there, a savage went back as
we supposed to fire the buildings. Farnsworth proposed to my husband to go back
with him, to get a quantity of pork from the
cellar, to help us on our journey; but Mr.
Johnson prudently replied, that by that
means, the Indians might find the rum, and
in a fit of intoxication kill us all. The Indian
presently returned with marks of fear in his
countenance,* and we were hurried on with
all violence. Two savages laid hold of each
of my arms, and hurried me through thorny
thickets, in a most unmerciful manner. I lost

---

*This, as we afterwards found, was occasioned by his
meeting Mr. Osmer at the door of the house, who lodged
in the chamber, and had secreted himself behind a
box, and was then making his escape. He run directly
to the fort, and the alarm guns were fired. My father,
Mr. Moses Willard, was then second in command.
Capt. Stevens was for sallying out with a party for our
relief; but my father begged him to desist, as the Indians made it an invariable practice to kill their prisoners when attacked.

a shoe and suffered exceedingly. We heard the alarm guns from the fort. This added new speed to the flight of the savages. They were apprehensive that soldiers might be sent for our relief. When we had got a mile and a half, my faintness obliged me to sit. This being observed by an Indian, he drew his knife, as I supposed, to put an end to my existence. But he only cut some bands with which my gown was tied, and then pushed me on. My little children were crying, my husband and the other two men were bound, and my sister and myself were obliged to make the best of our way, with all our might. The loss of my shoe rendered travelling extremely painful. At the distance of three miles there was a general halt; the savages, supposing that we, as well as themselves, might have an appetite for breakfast, gave us a loaf of bread, some raisins and apples, which they had taken from the house. While we were forcing down our scanty breakfast, a horse came in sight, known to us all by the name of Scoggin, belonging to Phinehas Stevens, Esquire. One of the Indians attempted to shoot him, but was prevented by Mr. Johnson. They then expressed a wish to catch him, saying, by pointing to me, for squaw to ride; my husband had previously been unbound to assist the children, he, with two Indians, caught the horse on the banks of the river. By this time my legs and feet were covered with blood, which being noticed by Mr. Labarree, he, with that humanity which never forsook him, took his own stockings and presented them to me, and the Indians gave me a pair of moggasons. Bags and blankets were thrown over Scoggin, and I mounted on the top of them, & on we jogged about seven miles, to the upper end of Wilcott's Island.—We there halted, and prepared to cross the river; rafts were made of dry timber—two Indians and Farnsworth crossed first—Labarree, by signs, got permission to swim the horse, and Mr. Johnson was allowed to swim by the raft that I was on, to push it along. We all arrived safe on the other side of the river, about four o'clock in the afternoon; a fire was kindled, and some of their stolen kettles were hung over it, and filled with porridge. The savages took delight in viewing their spoil, which amounted to forty or fifty pounds in value. They then, with a true savage yell, gave the war-whoop, and bid defiance to danger. As our tarry in this place lasted an hour, I had time to reflect on our miserable situation. Captives, in the power of unmerciful savages, without provision, and almost without clothes, in a wilderness where we must sojourn as long as the children of Israel did, for ought we knew, and what added to our distress, not one of our savage masters could understand a word of

English. Here, after being hurried from home with such rapidity, I have leisure to inform the reader respecting our Indian masters. They were eleven* in number, men of middle age, except one, a youth of sixteen, who in our journey discovered a very mischievous and troublesome disposition. According to their national practice, he who first laid hands on a prisoner, considered him as his property. My master, who was the one that took my hand when I sat on the bed, was as clever an Indian as I ever saw; he even evinced, at numerous times, a disposition that showed he was by no means void of compassion.—The four, who took my husband, claimed him as their property, and my sister, three children, Labarree and Farnsworth, had each a master. When the time came for us to prepare to march, I almost expired at the thought. To leave my aged parents, brothers, sisters and friends, and travel with savages, through a dismal forest to unknown regions, in the alarming situation I then was in, with three small children, the eldest, Sylvanus, who was but six years old.—My eldest daughter, Susanna, was four, and Polly, the

---

*Mr. Labarree is very positive, and I think Mr. Johnson was of the same opinion, that seventeen Indians attacked the house; the other six might have been a scouting party, that watched till we were out of danger, and then took another route.

other, two. My sister Miriam was fourteen. My husband was barefoot, and otherwise thinly clothed; his master had taken his jacket, and nothing but his shirt and trowsers remained. My two daughters had nothing but their shifts, and I only the gown that was handed me by the savages. In addition to the sufferings which arose from my own deplorable condition, I could not but feel for my friend Labarree; he had left a wife and four small children behind, to lament his loss, and to render his situation extremely unhappy. With all these misfortunes lying heavily upon me, the reader can imagine my situation. The Indians pronounced the dreadful word "munch," march, and on we must go. I was put on the horse, Mr. Johnson took one daughter, and Mr. Labarree, being unbound, took the other;—we went six or eight miles and stopped for the night. The men were made secure, by having their legs put in split sticks, somewhat like stocks, and tied with cords, which were tied to the limbs of trees too high to be reached. My sister, much to her mortification, must lie between two Indians, with a cord thrown over her, and passing under each of them; the little children had blankets, and I was allowed one for my use. Thus we took lodging for the night, with the sky for a covering, and the ground for a pillow. The fatigues of the preceding day obliged me to sleep several hours, in spite of the horrors which surrounded me. The Indians observed great silence, and never spoke but when really necessary, and all the prisoners were disposed to say but little; my children were much more peaceable than could be imagined—gloomy. fear imposed a deadly silence.

CHAP. II.

History of our Journey through the Wilderness, till we came to the waters that enter Lake Champlain.

IN the morning we were roused before sunrise, the Indians struck up a fire, hung on their stolen kettles, and made us some water gruel for breakfast. After a few sips of this meagre fare, I was again put on the horse, with my husband by my side to hold me on. My two fellow prisoners took the little girls, and we marched sorrowfully on for an hour or two, when a keener distress was added to my multiplied afflictions;—I was taken with the pangs of child-birth. The Indians signified to us that we must go on to a brook. When we got there, they shewed some humanity, by making a booth for me. Here the compassionate reader will drop a fresh tear, for my inexpressible distress; fifteen or twenty miles from the abode of any civilized being, in the open wilderness, rendered cold by a rainy day—in one of the most perilous hours, and unsupplied with the least necessary, that could yield convenience in the hazardous moment. My children were crying at a distance, where they were held by their masters, and only my husband and sister to attend me; none but

mothers can figure to themselves my unhappy
fortune. The Indians kept aloof the whole
time. About ten o'clock a daughter was born.*
They then brought me some articles of clothing for the child, which they had taken
from the house. My master looked into the
booth, and clapped his hands with joy, crying
two monies for me, two monies for me. I
was permitted to rest the remainder of the
day. The Indians were employed in making a

---

*In September, 1797, I made a tour, accompanied by
Elijah Grout, Esq., and my daughter, E. C. Kimball, to
Weathersfield, to find the spot of ground where my
daughter was born; but could not find it to my satisfaction at that time. In August, 1798, I again set off for
the same purpose, accompanied by my daughter aforesaid, and was joined by Nathaniel Stoton, Esq., and Mrs.
Whipple, of Weathersfield. In this tour we passed two
small streams, and on coming to the third I was convinced it must be up that stream some small distance. I
requested a halt; and on viewing a cliff of rocks, I informed my company that we were not far from the place.
The reader may well suppose that I was not a little
overjoyed at the expectation of viewing the place where I
had undergone so much sorrow. The keenest anguish
of soul, the providential deliverance, and the almost mirac-
ulous preservation, has ever rendered the recollection of
that spot dear to me, and it can only be forgotten with
my existence. We pursued up the stream a little far-
ther, and on viewing the rocks aforesaid, I knew them to
be the same which were spoken of by my husband and
others on the morning of our departure on our journey
with the Indians, which rock, they said, would remain
as a monument, that should any of us ever be so happy

bier for the prisoners to carry me on, and another booth for my lodging during night. They brought a needle and two pins, and some bark to tie the child's clothes, which they gave my sister, and a large wooden spoon to feed it with; at dusk they made some porridge, and brought a cup to steep some roots in, which Mr. Labarree had provided. In the evening I was removed to the new booth. For supper, they made more porridge and some

---

as to return, we might find the place; although at that time, it was nothing but a wilderness. We also discovered a small bog meadow where the horse mired with me in the morning prior to the birth of my child. And I recollected that it was nigh the brook, or when crossing the stream, that I felt the first pangs which were indicative of the sorrowful scene that soon followed. And from the rocks before mentioned, the bog meadows, the stream, and a dry spot of ground resembling the one on which the savages built my booth, *circumstances that could not well be forgotten*, I was very well satisfied as to its being the place for which I had sought. However, that I might be still more certain, (as I purposed to have a monument erected on the spot,) in 1799 I again set out, accompanied by my friend and fellow prisoner, Mr. Labarree, and took a further view, to ascertain with more precision the memorable place. When we had arrived we were both agreed as to the identical spot of ground, even within a few feet; and ascertained that it was on the northeast corner lot of land in Cavendish, and is about half a mile from the main road leading from Weathersfield to Reading, where is erected a monument with the following inscription—which the friendly reader may peruse if he should ever pass that way:

johnny cakes. My portion was brought me in a little bark. I slept that night far beyond expectation.

In the morning we were summoned for the journey, after the usual breakfast, of meal and water. I with my infant in my arms, was laid on the litter, which was supported alternately by Mr. Johnson, Labarree and Farnsworth.— My sister and son were put upon Scoggin, and

---

"This is near the spot where the Indians encamped the night after they took Mr. Johnson and family, Mr. Labarree and Farnsworth, August 30, 1754; and Mrs. Johnson was delivered of her child half a mile up this brook.

"When trouble's near the Lord is kind,
    He hears the captive's cry;
He can subdue the savage mind,
    And learn it sympathy."

Another monument is erected on the spot of ground where the child was born, with this inscription:—

"On the 31st of August, A. D. 1754, Capt. James Johnson had a daughter born on this spot of ground; being captivated with his whole family by the Indians.

"If mothers e'er should wander here,
    They'll drop a sympathetic tear
For her, who in the howling wild,
    Was safe deliver'd of a child."

In June, 1808, I, for the last time, visited the place where almost fifty-four years before, I had experienced the keenest sorrow that perhaps was ever equalled by any woman. I was accompanied by Col. Kimball and my daughter, E. Captive, his wife, to Weathersfield; and there we were joined by Capt. Sherwin and his wife, & Mr. Demell Grout. (This Mr. Demell Grout was a son of Mrs. Grout who was in captivity at the same time

the two little girls rode on their masters' backs. Thus we proceeded two miles, when my carriers grew too faint to proceed any further.— This being observed by our sable masters, a general halt was called, and they embodied themselves for council. My master soon made signs to Mr. Johnson that if I could ride on the horse I might proceed, otherwise I must be

---

that I was; and his given name was to keep in remembrance the name of the gentleman who bought his mother from the Indians, and was ever kind and friendly to her.) When we arrived at the brook, my thoughts were instantly back at the time I first saw it, though the scene was widely different from what it then was. It was then a dreary wilderness; now the wilderness was turned into fruitful fields, dressed in verdure, which richly repaid the labors of the husbandman. It was then a dwelling for savages and wild beasts of the forest; now a habitation of good citizens, with their flocks and herds, who live in domestic peace, happiness and plenty. After viewing the scene, and contemplating on the striking contrast a few moments, to add to the sensibility, we sat down and partook of a repast, and regaled ourselves with liquor mixed with water from the same fountain that I & my child first partook of in that gloomy and sorrowful day of trouble and affliction. Then my fare was meagre meal and water, and steeped roots, and a large *wooden spoon* to feed my infant babe; now we had the best of liquid spirits, and eatables, which in comparison, might be said to be dainties. The contrast is too great for pen to describe. My female readers, who are mothers, may in some degree conceive of it, though they cannot realize it like her to whom it is by experience a striking reality.

left behind. Here I observed marks of pity in his countenance, but this might arise from the fear of losing his two monies. I preferred an attempt to ride on the horse, rather than to perish miserably alone. Mr. Labarree took the infant, and every step of the horse almost deprived me of life. My weak and helpless condition rendered me, in a degree, insensible to every thing; my poor child could have no sustenance from my breast, and was supported entirely by water gruel. My other little children, rendered peevish by an uneasy mode of riding, often burst into cries, but a surly check from their masters soon silenced them. We proceeded on with a slow, mournful pace.—My weakness was too severe to allow me to sit on the horse long at a time; every hour I was taken off, and laid on the ground to rest. This preserved my life during the third day. At night we found ourselves at the head of Black River Pond. Here we prepared to spend the night, our supper consisted of gruel and the broth of a hawk, they had killed the preceding day. The prisoners were secured as usual, a booth was made for me, and all went to rest. After encampment, we entered into a short conversation. My sister observed that if I could have been left behind, our trouble would have been seemingly nothing. My husband hoped by the assistance of providence, we should all be preserved. Mr. Labarree pitied his poor family—and Farnsworth summed the whole of his wishes, by saying, that if he could have got a layer of pork from the cellar, we should not be in fear of starvation. The night was uncommonly dark, and passed tediously off.

In the morning, half chilled with a cold fog, we were ordered from our places of rest, offered the lean fare of meal & water, and then prepared for the journey; every thing resembled a funeral procession. The savages preserved their gloomy sadness—the prisoners, bowed down with grief and fatigue, felt little disposition to talk; and the unevenness of the country, sometimes lying in miry plains, at others rising into steep and broken hills, rendered our passage hazardous and painful. Mr. Labarree kept the infant in his arms, and preserved its life. The fifth day's journey was an unvaried scene of fatigue. The Indians sent out two or three hunting parties, who returned without game. As we had in the morning consumed the last morsel of our meal, every one now began to be seriously alarmed; and hunger, with all its horrors, looked us earnestly in the face. At night, we found the waters that run into Lake

Champlain, which was over the height of land; before dark we halted, and the Indians, by the help of their punk, which they carried in horns, made a fire. They soon adopted a plan to relieve their hunger. The horse was shot, and his flesh was in a few moments broiling on embers, and they, with native gluttony, satiated their craving appetites. To use the term politeness, in the management of their repast, may be thought a burlesque, yet their offering the prisoners the best parts of the horse, certainly bordered on civility; an epicure could not have catered nicer slices, nor in that situation served them up with more neatness. Appetite is said to be the best sauce, yet our abundance of it did not render savory this novel steak. My children, however, eat too much, which made them very unwell for a number of days. Broth was made for me and my child, which was rendered almost a luxury by the seasoning of roots. After supper, countenances began to brighten; those who had relished the meal exhibited new strength, and those who had only snuffed its effluvia, confessed themselves regaled; the evening was employed in drying and smoking what remained, for future use. The night was a scene of distressing fears to me, and my extreme weakness had affected my mind to such a degree, that every difficulty appeared doubly terrible. By the assistance of Scoggin, I had been brought so far, yet so great was my debility, that every hour I was taken off and laid on the ground, to keep me from expiring. But now, alas! this conveyance was no more. To walk was impossible. Inevitable death, in the midst of woods, one hundred miles wide, appeared my only portion.

CHAP. III.

Continuation,—till our arrival at East Bay, in Lake Champlain.

IN the morning of the sixth day, the Indians exerted themselves to prepare one of their greatest dainties. The marrow bones of old Scoggin were pounded for a soup, and every root, both sweet and bitter, that the woods afforded, was thrown in to give it a flavor. Each one partook of as much as his feelings would allow. The war-whoop then resounded, with an infernal yell, and we began to fix for a march. My fate was unknown, till my master brought some bark, and tied my petticoats, as high as he supposed would be convenient for walking, and ordered me to "munch." With scarce strength to stand alone, I went on half a mile, with my little son and three Indians. The rest were advanced. My power to move then failed, the world grew dark, and I dropped down. I had sight enough to see an Indian lift his hatchet over my head, while my little son screamed,— "Ma'am do go, for they will kill you." As I fainted, my last thought was, that I should presently be in the world of spirits. When I awoke my master was talking angrily with the savage who had threatened my life. By

his gestures I could learn, that he charged
him with not acting the honorable part of a
warrior, by an attempt to destroy the prize of
a brother. A whoop was given for a halt.
My master helped me to the rest of the company, where a council was held, the result of
which was that my husband should walk by
my side, and help me along. This he did
for some hours, but faintness then overpowered me, and Mr. Johnson's tenderness
and solicitude, was unequal to the task of
aiding me further; another council was held:
—while in debate, as I lay on the ground,
gasping for breath, my master sprang towards
me, with his hatchet. My husband and
fellow prisoners grew pale at the sight, sus-
pecting that he by a single blow, would rid
themselves of so great a burthen as I was.
But he had yet too much esteem for his "two
monies." His object was to get bark from a
tree, to make a pack-saddle, for my conveyance on the back of my husband.—He took
me up and we marched in that form the rest
of the day. Mr. Labarree still kept my infant, Farnsworth carried one of the little girls,
and the other rode with her master; they were
extremely sick and weak, owing to the large
portion of the horse, which they eat; but if
they uttered a murmuring word, a menacing
frown from the savages, soon imposed silence.
None of the Indians were disposed to shew

insults of any nature, except the youngest, which I have before mentioned. He often delighted himself, by tormenting my sister, by pulling her hair, treading on her gown, and numerous other boyish pranks, which were provoking and troublesome. We moved on, faint and wearily, till night; the Indians then yelled their war-whoop, built a fire, and hung over their horse broth. After supper, my booth was built, as usual, and I reposed much better than I had the preceding nights.

In the morning, I found myself greatly restored. Without the aid of physicians, or physic, nature had began the cure of that weakness, to which she had reduced me, but a few days before. The reader will be tired of the repetition of the same materials for our meals; but if my feelings can be realized, no one will turn with disgust from a breakfast of steaks, which were cut from the thigh of a horse. After which, Mr. Johnson was ordered to take the infant, and go forward with part of the company. I "munched" in the rear till we came to a beaver pond, which was formed in a branch of Otter Creek. Here I was obliged to wade; when half way over, up to the middle in cold water, my little strength failed, and my power to speak or see left me. While motionless and stiffened, in the middle of the pond, I was perceived from the other side, by Mr. Johnson, who laid down the infant, and came to my assistance; he took me in his arms, and when the opposite side was gained, life itself had apparently forsaken me. The whole company stopped, and the Indians, with more humanity than I supposed them possessed of, busied themselves in making a fire, to warm me into life. The warm influence of the fire restored my exhausted strength, by degrees; and in two hours I was told to munch. The rest of the day I was carried by my husband.—In the middle of the afternoon, we arrived on the banks of one of the great branches of Otter Creek. Here we halted, and two savages, who had been on a hunting scout, returned with a duck; a fire was made, which was thrice grateful to my cold shivering limbs. Six days had now almost elapsed, since the fatal morn, in which we were taken, and by the blessing of that Providence, whose smiles give life to creation, we were still in existence.—My wearied husband, naked children, and helpless infant, formed a scene that conveyed severer pangs to my heart, than all the sufferings I endured myself. The Indians were sullen and silent, the prisoners were swollen with gloomy grief, and I was half the time expiring. After my feelings were a little quickened by warmth, my sad portion was brought in a bark, consisting of the duck's head, and a gill of broth. As I lifted the unsavory morsel with a trembling hand, to my mouth, I cast my thoughts back a few days, to a time when, from a board plentifully spread, in my own house, I eat my food with a merry heart. The wooden spoon dropped from my feeble hand. The contrast was too affecting. Seated on a ragged rock, beneath a hemlock, as I then was; emaciated by sickness, and surrounded by my weeping and distressed family, who were helpless prisoners, despair would have robbed me of life, had I not put my whole confidence in that Being who has power to save. Our masters began to prepare to ford the stream. I swallowed most of my broth, and was taken up by my husband. The river was very rapid, and passing dangerous. Mr. Labarree, when half over with my child, was tripped up by its rapidity, and lost the babe in the water; little did I expect to see the poor thing again, but he fortunately reached a corner of its blanket, and saved its life. The rest got safe to the other shore—another fire was built, and my sister dried the infant, and its clothes.

Here we found a proof of Indian sagacity, which might justly be supposed not to belong to a band of rambling barbarians. In their journey over to the Connecticut River, they had, in this place, killed a bear. The entrails were cleansed and filled with the fat of the animal, and suspended from the limb of a tree; by it was deposited a bag of flour, and some tobacco, all which was designed for future stores, when travelling that way. Nothing could have been offered more acceptable, than these tokens of Indian economy and prudence. The flour was made into pudding, and the bear grease sauce was not unrelishing. Broth was made, and well seasoned with snakeroot, and those who were fond of tobacco had each their share. The whole formed quite a sumptuous entertainment. But these savage dainties made no sensible addition to our quota of happiness. My weakness increased, my children were very unwell, and Mr. Johnson's situation was truly distressing. By travelling barefoot, over such a length of forest, and supporting me on his shoulders, his feet were rendered sore, beyond description. I cannot express too much gratitude, for Mr. Labarree's goodness. My infant was his sole charge, and he supported it, by pieces of the horse flesh, which he kept for its use, which by being first chewed in his own mouth, and then put into the child's, afforded it the necessary nutriment. After supper, my booth was made, the evening yell was sounded, and we encamped for the night. By this time the savages had relaxed part of their watchfulness, and began to be careless of our escaping. Labarree and Farnsworth were slightly bound, and my husband had all his liberty. My sister could sleep without her two Indian companions, and the whole company appeared less like prisoners.

In the morning of the eighth day, we were roused at sunrise. Although the early part of September is generally blessed with a serene sky, and a warm sun, yet we suffered exceedingly by the cold. The mornings were damp and foggy, and the lofty trees, and numerous mountains, often exclude the sun till noon. Our snakeroot broth, enriched with flour, made a rare breakfast, and gave a little strength to our exhausted limbs. Orders came to "munch." My poor husband took me upon the pack saddle, and we resumed our march. Long before night, despondency had strikingly pictured every countenance. My little son, who had performed the whole journey on foot was almost lifeless. Mr. Johnson was emaciated, and almost exhausted;—often he laid me on the ground to save his own life, and mine; for my weakness was too great to ride far, without requiring rest. While prostrate upon the earth, and able to speak, I often begged him to leave me there to end a life, which could last but a short time, and would take his with it, if he continued his exertions to save me; but the idea was too shocking, we continued our journey, in a slow sorrowful mood, till night.

Often did I measure a small distance for the sun to run, before I must bid it an eternal adieu. But the same Providence· who had brought us so far, and inclined our savage masters to mercy, continued my protector. Farnsworth carried me a small distance, and at last darkness put an end to our painful day's journey. After the customary refreshment, we went to rest. The night was terrible; the first part was Egyptian darkness, then thunder and lightening, and rain. On the cold earth, without a cover, our situation may be imagined, but not described. The Indians gave me an additional blanket for my use, and shewed some concern for my welfare; but it will ever stand first among modern miracles, that my life was spared.

The morning came, and a bright sun reanimated our drowned spirits. The whole company now resembled a group of ghosts, more than bodily forms. Little did I expect that the light of another day would witness my existence; sensible, that if my own sad diseases did not finish my existence, my husband would be reduced to the woful alternative, of either perishing with me, or leaving me in the woods to preserve his own life.— The horrid yell was given, which was a signal for preparation. Melancholy sat heavily on every countenance, and the tear of woe moistened the sickened cheek of every prisoner. In addition to famine and fatigue, so long a journey, without a shoe for defence, had lacerated and mangled every foot, to a shocking degree; travelling was keenly painful. The scanty breakfast was served up; as I was lifting my gill of broth to my cold lips, my master, with a rash hand, pulled it from me, and gave it to my husband, observing by signs, that he required all the sustenance, to enable him to carry me. I yielded, on the supposition that it was a matter of little consequence, whether any thing was bestowed to that body which must soon mingle with its original clay. With sorrow and anguish, we began the ninth day's journey. Before we proceeded far, the Indians signified to us, that we should arrive, before night, at east bay, on Lake Champlain. This was a cordial to our drooping spirits, and caused an immediate transition from despair to joy; the idea of arriving at a place of water carriage, translated us to new life. Those who languished with sickness, fatigue or despair, now marched forward with nervous alacrity. Two Indians were sent on a hunting scout, who were to meet us at the Bay, with canoes. This seasonable and agreeable intelligence, had every possible effect that was good; we walked with greater speed, felt less of the journey, and thought little of our distress. About the middle of the afternoon the waters of the Lake were seen, from a neighboring eminence; we soon gained the bank, where we found the two Indians, with four canoes, and a ground squirrel; a fire was built, and some food put in preparation. Here my feelings, which had not been exhilarated so much as the rest of my fellow prisoners, were buoyed above despair, and, for a short time, the pangs of distress lost their influence. The life, which nine days painful suffering in the wilderness, had brought to its last moment of duration, now started into new existence, and rendered the hour I sat on the shore of Lake Champlain, one of the happiest I ever experienced. Here we were to take passage, in boats, and find relief from the thorny hills and miry swamps of the damp desert. My husband could now be relieved from the burden, which had bro't him as nigh eternity as myself. My little children would soon find clothing, and all my fellow sufferers would be in a condition to attain some of life's conveniences. Twelve hours sailing would waft us to the settlements of civilized Frenchmen. Considering how much we had endured, few will deem it less than a miracle, that we were still among the living. My son, of six years old, had walked barefoot the whole journey. Farnsworth was shoeless, and carried my eldest daughter. Labarree had to carry and preserve the life of my infant. My sister, owing to her youth and health, had suffered the least. My two little daughters, with only their shifts, and part of one of the three gowns, which the savage gave me, were subject to all the damps of morn and night; and Mr. Johnson's situation was pitiably painful; the fatigue of carrying me on the wearying pack saddle, had rendered his emaciated body almost a corpse, and his sore feet made him a cripple. The Indians had been surprisingly patient, and often discovered tokens of humanity. At every meal we all shared equal with them, whether a horse or a duck composed the bill of fare, and more than once they gave me a blanket, to shelter me from a thunder storm.

CHAP. IV.

*Crossing the Lake to Crown Point, from thence
to St. Johns, Chamblee, and to St. Francis
Village.*

I WILL only detain the reader a few
moments longer in this place, while I eat the
leg of a woodchuck, and then request him to
take a night's sailing in the canoe with me
across the Lake. Though I sincerely wish
him a better passage than I had. No sooner
was our repast finished, than the party were
divided into four equal parties, for passage.
In my boat were two savages, besides my son
and infant. I was ordered to lie flat on the
bottom of the canoe, and when pain obliged
me to move for relief, I had a rap from a pad-
dle. At day break, we arrived at a great
rock, on the west side of the Lake, where
we stopped and built a fire. The Indians
went to a French house, not far distant, and
got some meat, bread, and green corn. Although we were not allowed to taste the meat,
yet, by the grateful effluvia of the broiling
steak, we were finely regaled, and the bread
and roast corn, were a luxury.

Here the savages, for the first time, gave
loud tokens of joy, by hallooing and yelling
in a tremendous manner. The prisoners

were now introduced to a new school. Little did we expect that the accomplishment of dancing would ever be taught us, by the savages. But the war dance must now be held; and every prisoner that could move must take its awkward steps. The figure consisted of circular motion round the fire; each sang his own music, and the best dancer was the one most violent in motion. The prisoners were taught each a song, mine was, danna witchee natchepung; my son's was nar wiscumpton. The rest I cannot recollect. Whether this task was imposed on us for their diversion, or a religious ceremonial, I cannot say, but it was very painful and offensive. In the forenoon, seven Indians came to us, who were received with great joy by our masters, who took great pleasure in introducing their prisoners. The war dance was again held; we were obliged to join, and sing our songs, while the Indians rent the air with infernal yelling. We then embarked and arrived at Crown Point about noon. Each prisoner was then led by his master to the residence of the French commander. The Indians kept up their infernal yelling the whole time. We were ordered to his apartment, and used with that hospitality which characterizes the best part of the nation. We had brandy in profusion, a good dinner, and a change of linen. This was luxury indeed, after what we had suffered, for the want of these things. None but ourselves could prize their value. We, after dinner, were paraded before Mr. Commander, and underwent examination, after which we were shewn a convenient apartment, where we resided four days, not subject to the jurisdiction of our savage masters. Here we received great civilities, and many presents. I had a nurse, who in a great measure restored my exhausted strength. My children were all decently clothed, and my infant in particular. The first day, while I was taking a nap, they dressed it so fantastically, a la France, that I refused to own it, when brought to my bedside, not guessing that I was the mother of such a strange thing.

On the fourth day, to our great grief and mortification, we were again delivered to the Indians, who led us to the water side, where we all embarked in one vessel for St. Johns. The wind shifted, after a short sail, and we dropped anchor. In a little time a canoe came along side of us, in which was a white woman, who was bound for Albany. Mr. Johnson begged her to stop a few minutes, while he wrote to Col. Lydius of Albany, to inform him of our situation, and to request him to put the same in the Boston newspapers, that our friends might learn that we were alive. The woman delivered the letter, and the contents were published, which conveyed the agreeable tidings to our friends, that although prisoners, we were then alive.

The following letter, in return for the one we sent to Col. Lydius, was the first we received from New-England: ·

ALBANY, NOV. 5, 1754.

SIR—I received yours of the 5th October, with a letter or two for New-England, which I have forwarded immediately, and have wrote to Boston, in which I urged the government to endeavor your and family's redemption as soon as conveniency would admit.

I am quite sorry for your doleful misfortune, and hope the just God will endue you with patience to undergo your troubles, and justly use his rewards on the evil doers and authors of your misfortune.—Present my service to all the prisoners with you, from him who subscribes himself to be your very humble servant,

JOHN W. LYDIUS.

Lieut. James Johnson, Montreal.

After a disagreeable voyage of three days, we made St. Johns, the 16th of September, where we again experienced the politeness of a French commander. I with my child, was kindly lodged in the same room with himself and lady. In the morning we still found misfortune treading close at our heels;—we must again be delivered to our savage masters, and take another passage in the boats for Chamblee, when within three miles of which, Labarree, myself and child, with our two masters, were put on shore; we were ignorant of our destiny, and parting from my husband and friends, was a severe trial, without knowing whether we were ever to meet them again. We walked on to Chamblee; here our fears were dissipated, by meeting our friends. In the garrison of this place, we found all the hospitality our necessities required. Here for the first, after my captivity, I lodged on a bed. Brandy was handed about in large bowls, and we lived in high style. The next morning we were put in the custody of our old masters, who took us to the canoes, in which we had a painful voyage that day, and the following night to Sorell, where we arrived on the 19th. A hospitable friar came to the shore to see us, and invited us to his house; he gave us a good breakfast, and drank our better healths, in a tumbler of brandy; he took compassionate notice of my child, and ordered it some suitable food. But the Indians hurried us off before it could eat. He then went with us to the shore, and ordered his servant to carry the food, prepared for the child, to the canoe, where he waited till I fed it. The friar was a very genteel man, and gave us his benediction, at parting, in feeling language.

We then rowed on till the middle of the afternoon, when we landed on a barren heath, and by the help of a fire, cooked an Indian dinner, after which the war dance was held, and another infernal yelling. The prisoners were obliged to sing, till they were hoarse, and dance round the fire.

We had now arrived within a few miles of the village of St. Francis, to which place our masters belonged. Whenever the warriors return from an excursion against an enemy, their return to the tribe or village must be designated by warlike ceremonial; the captives or spoil, which may happen to crown their valor, must be conducted in a triumphant form, and decorated to every possible advantage.—For this end we must now submit to painting; their vermillion, with which they were ever supplied, was mixed with bear's grease, and every cheek, chin and forehead must have a dash. We then rowed on within a mile of the town, where we stopped at a French house, to dine; the prisoners were served with soup meagre and bread. After dinner, two savages proceeded to the village, to carry the glad tidings of our arrival. The whole atmosphere soon resounded from every quarter, with whoops, yells, shrieks and screams. St. Francis, from the noise that came from it, might be supposed the centre of Pandemonium. Our masters were not backward, they made every response they possibly could. The whole time we were sailing from the French house, the noise was direful to be heard. Two hours before sunset, we came to the landing, at the village. No sooner had we landed, than the yelling in the town was redoubled; a cloud of savages, of all sizes and sexes, soon appeared running towards us; when they reached the boats, they formed themselves into a long parade, leaving a small space, through which we must pass. Each Indian then took his prisoner by his hand, and after ordering him to sing the war song, began to march thro' the gauntlet. We expected a severe beating, before we got through, but were agreeably disappointed, when we found that each Indian only gave us a tap on the shoulder. We were led directly to the houses, each taking his prisoner to his own wigwam. When I entered my master's door, his brother saluted me with a large belt of wampum, and my master presented me with another. Both were put over my shoulders, and crossed behind and before. My new home was not the most agreeable; a large wigwam without a floor, with a fire in the centre, and only a few water vessels and dishes, to eat from, made of birch bark, and tools for cookery made clumsily of wood, for furniture, will not be thought a pleasing residence to one accustomed to civilized life.

CHAP. V.

Residence at St. Francis. Sale of most of the Prisoners to the French, and Removal to Montreal.

NIGHT presently came, after our arrival at St. Francis. Those who have felt the gloomy, homesick feelings, which sadden those hours which a youth passes, when first from a father's house, may judge of part of my sufferings; but when the rest of my circumstances are added, their conception must fall infinitely short. I now found myself, with my infant, in a large wigwam, accompanied with two or three warriors, and as many squaws, where I must spend the night, and perhaps a year.—My fellow prisoners were dispersed over the town; each one, probably, feeling the same gloominess with myself. Hasty pudding presently was brought forward for supper. A spacious bowl of wood, well filled, was placed in a central spot, and each one drew near with a wooden spoon. As the Indians never use seats, nor have any in their wigwams, my awkwardness in taking my position, was a matter of no small amusement to my new companions.—The squaws first fall upon their knees, and then sit back upon their heels. This was a posture that I could not imitate. To sit in any other was

thought by them indelicate and unpolite.
But I advanced to my pudding with the best
grace I could, not, however, escaping some
of their funny remarks. When the hour for
sleep came on, for it would be improper to
call it bed time, where beds were not, I was
pointed to a platform, raised half a yard,
where upon a board, covered with a blanket,
I was to pass the night. The Indians threw
themselves down in various parts of the building, in a manner that more resembled cows,
in a shed, than human beings, in a house. In
the morning, our breakfast consisted of the
relicks of the last night; my sister came to
see me in the forenoon, and we spent some
hours, in observations upon our situation,
while washing some apparel, at a brook. In
the afternoon, I with my infant, was taken to
the grand parade, where we found a large
collection of the village inhabitants; an aged
chief stepped forward, into an area, and after
every noise was silenced, and every one fixed
in profound attention, he began to harrangue;
his manner was solemn—his motions and
expression gave me a perfect idea of an orator. Not a breath was heard, & every spec-
tator seemed to reverence what he said.
After the speech, my little son was brought
to the opposite side of the parade, and a
number of blankets laid by his side. It now
appeared that his master and mine intended

an exchange of prisoners. My master being a hunter, wished for my son, to attend him on his excursions. Each delivered his property with great formality; my son and blankets, being an equivalent for myself, child and wampum. I was taken to the house of my new master, and found myself allied to the first family; my master, whose name was Gill, was son-in-law to the grand sachem, was accounted rich, had a store of goods, and lived in a style far above the majority of his tribe.—He often told me that he had an English heart, but his wife was true Indian blood. Soon after my arrival at his house, the interpreter came to inform me that I was adopted into his family. I was then introduced to the family, and was told to call them brothers and sisters, I made a short reply, expressive of gratitude, for being introduced to a house of high rank, and requested their patience while I should learn the customs of the nation. This was scarce over when the attention of the village was called to the grand parade, to attend a rejoicing occasioned by the arrival of some warriors, who had brought some scalps. They were carried in triumph on a pole. Savage butchery, upon murdered countrymen! The sight was horrid! As I retired to my new residence, I could hear the savage yells that accompanied the war dance. I spent the night in sad reflection.

My time now was solitary beyond description; my new sisters and brothers treated me with the same attention that they did their natural kindred, but it was an unnatural situation to me. I was a novice at making canoes, bunks, and tumplines, which was the only occupation of the squaws; of course, idleness was among my calamities. My fellow prisoners were as gloomy as myself; ignorant whether they were to spend their days in this inactive village, or be carried into a war campaign, to slaughter their countrymen, or to be dragged to the cold Lakes of the north, in a hunting voyage. We visited each other daily, and spent our time in conjecturing our future destiny.

The space of forty-two years having elapsed since my residence in St. Francis, it is impossible to give the reader a minute detail of events that occurred while there; many of them are still forcibly impressed upon my memory, but dates and particulars are now inaccurately treasured up by faint recollection. Mr. Johnson tarried but a few days with me before he was carried to Montreal to be sold. My two daughters, sister and Labarree, were soon after carried to the same place, at different times. Farnsworth was carried by his master, on a hunting scout, but not proving so active in the chase and ambush as they wished, he was returned and sent to Montreal.

I now found an increase to my trouble, with only my son and infant, in this strange land, without a prospect of relief, and with all my former trouble lying heavy upon me disappointment and despair came well nigh being my executioners. In this dilemma, who can imagine my distress, when my little son came running to me one morning, swollen with tears, exclaiming, that the Indians were going to carry him into the woods to hunt; he had scarcely told the piteous story, before his master came, to pull him away; he threw his little arms around me, begging in the agony of grief, that I would keep him. The inexorable savage unclenched his hands, and forced him away; the last words I heard, intermingled with his cries, were, Ma'am I shall never see you again. The keenness of my pangs almost obliged me to wish that I never had been a mother. Farewell, Sylvanus, said I, God will preserve you.

It was now the 15th of October.—Forty five days had passed since my captivity, and no prospect but what was darkened with clouds of misfortune. The uneasiness occasioned by indolence, was in some measure relieved, by the privilege of making shirts for my brother. At night and morn I was allowed to milk the cows. The rest of the time I strolled gloomily about, looking sometimes into an unsociable wigwam, at others sauntering into the bushes, and walking on the banks of brooks. Once I went to a French house, three miles distant, to visit some friends of my brother's family, where I was entertained politely a week; at another time, I went with a party to fish, accompanied by a number of squaws. My weakness obliged me to rest often, which gave my companions a poor opinion of me; but they shewed no other resentment, than calling me "no good squaw," which was the only reproach my sister ever gave, when I displeased her. All the French inhabitants I formed an acquaintance with, treated we with that civility which distinguishes the nation; once in particular, being almost distracted with an aching tooth, I was carried to a French physician, across the river, for relief. They prevailed on the Indians, to let me visit them a day or two, during which time, their marked attention and generosity claims my warmest gratitude. At parting, they expressed their earnest wishes to have me visit them again.

St. Francis contained about thirty wigwams which were thrown disorderly into a clump. There was a church, in which mass was held every night and morning, and every Sunday the hearers were summoned by a bell; and attendance was pretty general. Ceremonies were performed by a French friar, who lived in the midst of them for the salvation of their souls. He appeared to be in that place, what the legislative branch is in civil governments, and the grand sachem the executive. The inhabitants lived in perfect harmony, holding most of their property in common. They were prone to indolence, when at home, and not remarkable for neatness. They were extremely modest, and apparently averse to airs of courtship. Necessity was the only thing that called them to action; this induced them to plant their corn, and to undergo the fatigues of hunting. Perhaps I am wrong to call necessity the only motive; revenge, which prompts them to war, has great power. I had a numerous retinue of relations, whom I visited daily; but my brother's house, being one of the most decent in the village, I fared full as well at home. Among my connexions was a little brother Sabatis, who brought the cows for me, and took particular notice of my child. He was a sprightly little fellow, and often amused me with feats performed with his bow and arrow.

In the early part of November, Mr. Johnson wrote from Montreal, requesting me to prevail on the Indians to carry me to Montreal, for sale, as he had made provision for that purpose. I disclosed the matter, which was agreed to by my brother and sister, and on the seventh we set sail in a little bark canoe. While crossing Lake St. Peters, we came nigh landing on the shores of eternity. The waves were raised to an enormous height by the wind, and often broke over the canoe. My brother and sister were pale as ghosts, and we all expected immediate destruction; but the arm of salvation was extended for our relief, and we reached the shore. We were four days in this voyage, and received obliging civilities every night, at French settlements; on the eleventh, we arrived at Montreal, where I had the supreme satisfaction of meeting my husband, children, and friends. Here I had the happiness to find, that all my fellow prisoners had been purchased, by persons of respectability, by whom they were treated with humanity; and all except Polly, of whom I shall say something further, I believe were used very well.

Mr. Du Quesne bought my sister, my eldest daughter was owned by three affluent old maids, by the name of Jaisson, and the other, to wit, Polly, was owned by the mayor of the city. The mayor's lady had her kept out at boarding and nursing. I had information that the child was not well used; that no proper care was taken of her. I set off with a determination to find her, which I did, and on finding her, I found the intelligence which I had received but too true. To see my child in so miserable a plight gave my mind much trouble. I informed those where she was kept that I could not think of having her kept in such a manner, and should endeavor to have her taken away, and put where she might have better care taken of her. I went not long after to see her again, but was forbid to see her, by order of the mayor's lady. I thought it very hard that I could not be suffered to see my unhappy child, and was determined, if possible, to get her away. On my returning to my lodging, I immediately went with an interpreter to see the lady. It was with much difficulty that I could even get admittance so as to speak to her; but when I did, I collected all my fortitude, and in the feeling language of a mother, made my suit for liberty to visit my child. But I was denied with a frown! The lady could not see why a poor woman, and a prisoner, as I was, should want to torment herself and the child with such fruitless visits! She said that the child was well enough off, and when it arrived at a suitable age she should see to it herself! But I expostulated with her, by the interpreter, upbraided her with her cruelty and hardheartedness, and the vanity of her thinking, because I was poor, I had not, or need not have, any love or concern for my child! I requested her to think as a mother, that poverty did not, nor could it ever, erase parental love and affection. I told her that the child was mine, and she had no right to it. We were prisoners it was true, but I expected we should be exchanged, when I expected that I and my children would return to our native country. I conjured her to think of me on her pillow, and realize the matter, by making my case hers, and consider what torture I must be in, while, in addition to my being a poor prisoner, I was deprived of the privilege of seeing my poor unhappy child. And much more I said to her, to this effect, to which she seemed to pay some attention, but gave me no favorable answer. I returned to my lodging, rather sad and gloomy, though not entirely out of hopes but what I should finally meet with success; for I thought that the lady (and a lady indeed she appeared to be) must be lost to all sense of humanity, or else I must have wrought a little upon her feelings, which was my object to do. And in this I was not disappointed; for the next day she sent her servant to the interpreter for to inform me that I might see my child, and do with it according to my wishes. "Tell that English woman," said she, "I could not sleep last night; her observations broke my heart! She may have her child! I cannot withhold it from her any longer!" And she was as good as her word; for she furnished clothing, and I had my dear little child to myself, and had several presents with it from the lady, and she asked nothing for all her trouble.

I would remark here, that is was fashionable among the higher class of people in Canada, to have their own children nursed out till they were about three or four years old. They are dressed neat and clean about once a month, and carried to their parents, by the servant, to visit. The other part of the time they are not kept in so clean a manner by their nurses as the English people generally are. And perhaps mine was more neglected for being a poor prisoner's child. I also learned that the mayor's lady wished very much to have my child again, for her own, as she had had but only one daughter, who had died just before, aged 15 years.

But to return again to my narrative——Mr. Johnson had obtained the privilege of two months' absence on parole, for the purpose of going to New-England, to procure cash for the redemption of his family; he sat out on his journey the day after my arrival at Montreal. Mr. Du Quesne engaged to supply his family with necessaries, during his absence, and was to be recompensed at his return. Directly after his departure, I found myself doomed to fresh trouble. The Indians brought me here for the purpose of exchanging me for some Micanaw savages, a tribe with whom they were at war; but being disappointed in this, they were exorbitant in their demands, and refused to take less than

a thousand livres for me and my child. Mr.
Du Quesne fixed his offer at seven hundred,
which was utterly refused by my savage masters. Their next step was to threaten to carry
me back to St. Francis. After half a day's
surly deliberation, they concluded to take the
offered sum. I was received into Mr. Du
Quesne's family. My joy at being delivered
from savage captivity was unbounded. From
this period, Indians and sufferings were no
more to torture me, or my family, except the
unfortunate Sylvanus. The fond idea of
liberty, held forth its dazzling pleasures, and
the ignorance of future calamities, precluded
every cloud, that could obscure its effulgence.
On Mr. Johnson's journey to New-England
I rested all my hope, and felt full confidence
in being relieved at his return.

In justice to the Indians, I ought to remark,
that they never treated me with cruelty to a
wanton degree; few people have survived a
situation like mine, and few have fallen into
the hands of savages disposed to more lenity
and patience. Modesty has ever been a characteristic of every savage tribe; a truth which
my whole family will join to corroborate, to
the extent of their knowledge. As they are
aptly called the children of nature, those who
have profited by refinement and education,
ought to abate part of the prejudice, which
prompts them to look with an eye of censure

on this untutored race. Can it be said of civilized conquerors, that they, in the main, are willing to share with their prisoners, the last ration of food, when famine stares them in the face? Do they ever adopt an enemy, and salute him by the tender name of brother? And I am justified in doubting, whether if I had fallen into the hands of French soldiery, so much assiduity would have been shewn, to preserve my life.

CHAP. VI.

Mr. Johnson's Tour to Boston and Portsmouth, and the Catastrophe at his return. Arrival at the Prison in Quebec.

THE reader will leave me and my family, under the care of our factor, a short time, and proceed with Mr. Johnson. On the 12th of November, he sat out for Albany, accompanied by two Indians for pilots, for whose fidelity the commander in chief was responsible.— They were to tarry at Albany till his return. In a short time I had a letter from Col. Lydius, informing me that he had safely arrived at Albany, and had gone to Boston. His first step was to apply to Governor Shirley, for money to redeem his family, and the English prisoners. Shirley laid his matter before the General Assembly, and they granted the sum of ten pounds, to defray his expenses. He got no further assistance in Massachusetts, and was advised to apply to the government of New-Hampshire. Gov. Wentworth laid the matter before the General Assembly of that state, and the sum of one hundred and fifty pounds sterling was granted for the purpose of redemption of prisoners. The committee of the General Court of New-Hampshire gave him the following directions:

Portsmouth, N. H., Jan. 25, 1755.
MR. JAMES JOHNSON—SIR,

Agreeable to your letter to the Secretary, of the 16th instant, you have enclosed a letter to Col. Cornelius Cuyler, Esq. in which you will observe we have given you credit, for letters on his acquaintance in Canada, to furnish you with credit, to the amount of 150 pounds sterling. We therefore advise you to proceed to Albany, and on your arrival there, deliver the said letter to Col. Cuyler, and take from him such credit as he shall give you, on some able person or persons in Canada, and when you are thus furnished, you will then proceed to Canada, and there negociate, in the best and most frugal manner you can, the purchasing such, and so many captives, as you may hear of, that have been taken from any part of this province, taking care that the aforesaid sum agreeable to the grant of the General Assembly here, be distributed, to and for the purchasing all the said captives, that are to be come at, in the most equal and exact manner, that none may be left there for want of their quota of said money. The captives' names, and places from whence taken, that we have information of, you have herewith a list of, for your direction. You are to keep an exact account of the distribution of this money, in order to your future discharge.

If Colonel Cuyler should not be living, or

refuse you his good offices in this affair, you are then to apply to the Hon. ——— Saunders, Esq. Mayor of the city of Albany, or any other person that can give you credit at Canada, and leave with them our letter to Col. Cuyler, which shall oblige us to pay the said sum or sums, mentioned in the said letter, to such person, and in the same way and manner, as we have obliged ourselves to pay him.

We are your friends,

THEODORE ATKINSON, ⎫
S. WIBIRT, ⎪
MESHECH WEARE, ⎬ *Com.*
BENJ. SHERBURNE, jun. ⎭

A List of the Captives, taken from the Province of New-Hampshire, by the St. Francis Indians, in the summer of 1754.

From Charlestown, on Connecticut River, James Johnson, his wife, and four children.

Peter Labarree.

Ebenezer Farnsworth.

Miriam Willard.

From Merrimack River, .

Nathaniel Mallon, his wife and three children.

Robert Barber.

Samuel Scribner.

Enos Bishop.

In addition to this letter of credit, Governor Wentworth gave him the following passport:

Province of New-Hampshire, in New-England.

By His Excellency BENNING WENTWORTH, Esq. Captain General, Governor, and Commander in Chief, in and over his Britannic Majesty's Province of New-
L. S. Hampshire aforesaid, and Vice Admiral of the same, and Surveyor General of all his Majesty's Woods, in North America:

WHEREAS the St. Francis and other Indians did, in the summer last past, captivate sundry of his Majesty's subjects, inhabitants of this Province, and have, as I have been informed, sold the same to the subjects of the French King in Canada, where they are now detained in servitude; and having had application made to me, by Mr. James Johnson, of Charlestown, within this Province, one of the said captives, who obtained leave to come to this country, in order to purchase his own, and other captives' liberty. For letters of safe passport, I do hereby require and command, all officers, civil and military, as well as all other persons, that they offer no lett or hindrance to the said James Johnson, or his company, but contrarywise, that they afford him all necessary dispatch in said journey through this Province.

And I do hereby also desire, that all his Majesty's subjects, of his several other governments, through which the said Johnson may have occasion to travel, may treat him with that civility that becometh.

I also hereby earnestly entreat the Governor General, and all other officers, ministers and subjects of his most Christian Majesty, governing and inhabiting the country and territories of Canada aforesaid, that they would respectively be aiding and assisting to the said James Johnson, in the aforesaid negociation. Hereby engaging to return the same civility and kindness, to any of his most Christian Majesty's officers and subjects, when thereto requested, by any of his Governors or proper officers. In token of which, I have caused the public seal of the Province of New-Hampshire aforesaid, to be hereunto affixed, this 25th day of January, in the 28th year of the reign of our Sovereign Lord George the Second, of Great Britain, France, and Ireland, King, Defender of the Faith, &c.

BENNING WENTWORTH.

By his Excellency's Command,
THEODORE ATKINSON, Sec'y.
Anno Domini 1755.

With these credentials, Mr. Johnson proceeded with alacrity to Boston, procured Gov. Shirley's passport, and set forward to Worcester, on his return back: while there, he was greatly astonished at receiving the following letter from Governor Shirley:

Boston, February 15, 1755.

MR. JOHNSON,

There have some things happened in our public affairs, since your going from Boston, with my letters to the Governor of Canada, and intelligence come of the motions of the French in Canada, for further invading his Majesty's territories on the frontiers of New-York and New-Hampshire, as make it unsafe for you, as well as for the public, to proceed at present on your journey to Quebec; and therefore I expect that you do forthwith, upon receiving this letter, return back, and lay aside all thoughts of going forward on this journey, till you have my leave, or the leave of Governor Wentworth, to whom I shall write, and inform him of what I have undertook to do in this matter, in which his Majesty's service is so much concerned.   W. SHIRLEY.

Mr. James Johnson.

On the receipt of this letter, he returned with a heavy heart to Boston, and was positively ordered by Shirley, to stay till further orders. His situation now was really deplorable. His parole, which was only for two months, must be violated; his credit in Canada lost; his family exposed to the malice of exasperated Frenchmen, and all his good prospects at an end. After using every exertion, in Boston, for leave to recommence his journey, and spending the rest of the winter, and all the spring, he found his efforts were in vain. During this time, my situation grew daily distressing. Mr. Du Quesne made honorable provision for myself, sister and child, till the expiration of my husband's parole; the two Indians were then sent to Albany, to pilot him back; after waiting some time, and learning nothing about him, they returned. Previous to this I had been treated with great attention and civility; dined frequently in the first families, received cards to attend them on parties of pleasure, and was introduced to a large and respectable acquaintance. As an unfortunate woman, I received those general tokens of generosity which flow from a humane people. Among the presents which I received was one of no small magnitude, from Captains Stowbrow and Vambram, two gentlemen who were delivered by Major Washington, as hostages, when he, with the Virginia troops, surrendered to the French and Indians. In compliance with their billet, I waited on them one morning, and at parting received a present of 148 livres. Mr. St. Agne, a French gentleman of fortune and distinction, beside frequent proofs of his goodness, gave me at one time 48 livres. In his family I formed an intimate acquaintance with a young English lady who was captured by the Indians in the Province of Maine, and sold to him: She was used with parental tenderness, and shared the privileges of his children; she, with his daughter, frequently came in their morning carriage, to ride with my sister and me. Gratitude to my numerous benefactors, pleads loudly in favor of inserting all their names, and particularizing every act of generosity. If I omit it, it must not be imagined that I have forgotten their charity; it has left an impression on my heart, that can only be erased with my existence.

While in Mr. Du Quesne's family, my little daughter was very unwell, and the superstitious people were convinced that she would either die, or be carried off by the Devil, unless baptized. I yielded to their wishes, and they prepared for the ceremony, with all the appendages annexed to their religion. Mr. Du Quesne was godfather, and the young English lady godmother; by Mrs. Du Quesne's particular request, she was christened Louise, after herself—to which I added the name of Captive.

The return of the Indians, without Mr. Johnson, boded no good to me. I observed with pain, the gradual change in my friends, from coldness to neglect, and from neglect to contempt. Mr. Du Quesne, who had the most delicate sense of honor, supposed that he had designedly broken his parole, and abused his confidence; he refused to grant me further assistance, or even to see my face. I now found myself friendless and alone; not a word had I heard from Mr. Johnson, not a word had I heard from my little son, with the Indians. Affliction lowered upon me, with all its horrors; in this dilemma, my sister and I agreed to take a small room, and support ourselves, till our little store of cash was expended, and then have recourse to our needles.

In the beginning of April, the Indians made a second tour to Albany, in quest of Mr. Johnson, and again returned without him. I wrote to Col. Lydius for information, but he could tell nothing. Darkness increased; but I summoned all my resolution, and indulged the fond hope of being soon relieved. We kept our little room till June, when I had the happiness to hear that my husband was without the city, waiting for permission to come in. He was conducted in by a file of men; his presence banished care and trouble, and turned the tear of sorrow to the effusion of joy; after the joy of meeting had subsided, he related his sad fate in New England. He finally got permission from Gov. Wentworth to come privately, by the way of Albany, where he took his bills, drawn by Mr. Cuyler, on Mr. St. Luc Lucorne, and Mr. Rine Du Quesne. The face of affairs in Canada had materially changed; during his absence a new Governor had been sent over, and various manœuvres in politics had taken place, which were very injurious to him. Had the old governor tarried, his absence would have probably been excused. But Mons. Vaudrieul was ignorant of the conditions on which he went home, and could not admit apologies, for the breach of his parole. Our disappointment and mortification were severe, when we found our bills protested. This reduced us at once to a beggarly state. The evil was partially remedied by St. Luc Lucorne's lending us paper money, while we could send some Indians to Mr. Cuyler for silver. Mr. Johnson received orders to settle his affairs with all possible dispatch.

Spirited preparations were now making for war. General Dieskau arrived from France, with an army, and Montreal was a scene of busy confusion. We were completing our settlements, with our paper, expecting to have full permission to go home, when the Indians returned. But the measure of our misery was not yet full. In the beginning of July Mr. Johnson was put into jail. Terrible to me was this unexpected stroke; without money, credit or friends, I must now roam the streets, without a prospect of relief from the cloud of misfortune that hung over me. In a few days, the faithful Indians, who had been sent to Mr. Cuyler for the silver, returned, with 438 dollars, with an order on St. Luc Lucorne, for 700 additional livres; but he took the whole into possession, and we never after received a penny from him.

Half distracted, and almost exhausted with despair and grief, I went to the Governor, to paint our distress and ask relief. I found him of easy access, and he heard my lamentable story with seeming emotion; his only promise was to take care of us, and at parting he gave me a crown, to buy milk for my babes. Ignorant of our destiny, my sister and I kept our little room, and were fortunate enough to get subsistence from day to day—often going to the gloomy prison, to see my poor husband, whose misfortunes in Boston had brought him to this wretchedness.

Our own misfortunes had taught us how to feel for the sufferings of others, and large demands were now made on our sympathetic powers. Just as we were plunged into this new distress, a scout of savages brought a number of prisoners into Montreal, which were our old friends and acquaintance.* Our

---

*Two children from Mr. H. Grout's family, and two children belonging to Mrs. Howe, the fair captive, celebrated in Col. Humphrey's life of Putnam. Their names were Polly and Submit Phips. Mrs. Howe was then a prisoner at St. John's, with six other children, and one

meeting was a scene of sorrow and melancholy pleasure.

All were now flocking to the standard of war. The Indians came from all quarters, thirsting for English blood, and receiving instruction from the French. A number of tribes, with all their horrid weapons of war, paraded, one morning, before the General's house, and held the war dance, and filled the air with infernal yells; after which, in a formal manner, they took the hatchet against the English, and marched for the field of battle. Alas! my poor countrymen, thought I, how many of you are to derive misery from these monsters.

On the 22d of July, Mr. Johnson was taken from the jail, & with myself & our two youngest children, were ordered on board a vessel for Quebec. To leave our friends at Montreal, was a distressing affair; my sister's

---

Garfield. They were all taken at Hinsdale.—Mrs. Howe's daughters were purchased by Mons. Vaudrieul, the Governor, and had every attention paid their education. After a year's residence in Montreal, they were sent to the grand nunnery in Quebec, where my sister and I made them a visit; they were beautiful girls, cheerful and well taught. We here found two aged English ladies, who had been taken in former wars. One, by the name of Wheelright, who had a brother in Boston, on whom she requested me to call, if ever I went to that place; I complied with her request afterwards, and received many civilities from her brother.

ransom had been paid, but she could not go with us. She went into the family of the Lieut. Governor, where she supported herself with her needle. My eldest daughter was still with the three old maids, who treated her tenderly. Labarree and Farnsworth had paid the full price of their redemption, but were not allowed to go home. Not a word had we heard yet from poor Sylvanus. We parted in tears ignorant of our destination, but little thinking that we were to embark for a place of wretchedness and woe. After two days good sailing, we arrived at Quebec, and were all conducted directly to jail.

CHAP. VII.

*Six months residence in the Criminal Jail,
and removal to the Civil Prison.*

WE now, to our indescribable pain, found
the fallacy of Mr. Governor's promises, for
our welfare. This jail was a place too shocking for description. In one corner sat a poor
being, half dead with the small pox; in
another were some lousy blankets and straw;
in the centre stood a few dirty dishes, and the
whole presented a scene miserable to view.
The terrors of starvation, and the fear of suf-
focating in filth, were overpowered by the
more alarming evil of the small pox, which
none of us had had. But there was no retreat;
resignation was our only resource. The first
fortnight we waited anxiously for the attack
of the disease, in which time we were supported by a small piece of meat a day, which
was stewed with some rusty crusts of bread,
and brought to us in a pail that swine would
run from. The straw and lousy blankets were
our only lodging, and the rest of our furniture
consisted of some wooden blocks for seats.
On the fifteenth day I was taken with the
small pox, and removed to the hospital;
leaving my husband and two children in the
horrid prison. In two days Mr. Johnson put

my youngest child, Captive, out to nurse. The woman kept the child but a few days before she returned it, owing to a mistrust that she should not get her pay.

My husband brought the child to me at the hospital, and told me the sad tale. And after bathing the poor little infant in tears I thought and said, "the task is too hard—had it been the will of God to have taken the child away it might have alleviated some part of our trouble!" But my husband immediately checked my murmurings, and said, "be still and let us not complain of the providence of God; for we know not for what purpose this dear child is so miraculously preserved. It may yet be the greatest comfort to us in our old age should we arrive to it;" and much more he said to this effect, which I do not so particularly recollect. And I am constrained to say that I have had the happiness of finding his predictions fully exemplified. But to return to my narrative. Should the dear little thing remain in prison, certain death must inevitably be her portion. My husband was therefore reduced to the sad necessity of re- questing the woman to carry it to the Lord Intendant, and tell him that he must either allow her a compensation for keeping it, or it must be left at his door.—The good woman dressed it decently, and obeyed her orders. Mr. Intendant smiled at her story, and took the child in his arms, saying it was a pretty little English devil, it was a pity it should die; he ordered his clerk to draw an order for its allowance, and she took good care of it till the last of October, except a few days while it had the small pox.

A few days after I left the prison, Mr. Johnson and my other daughter were taken with symptoms and came to the hospital to me. It is a singular instance of Divine Interposition, that we all recovered from this malignant disease. We were remanded to prison, but were not compelled to our former rigid confinement. Mr. Johnson was allowed, at certain times, to go about the city, in quest of provision. But on the 20th of October, St. Luc Lucorne arrived from Montreal, with the news of Dieskau's defeat; he had ever since my husband's misfortune, about his parole, been his persecuting enemy. By his instigation we were all put directly to close prison.

The ravages of the small pox reduced us to the last extremity, and the fœtid prison, without fire and food, added bitterness to our distress. Mr. Johnson preferred a petition to the Lord Intendant, stating our melancholy situation. I had the liberty of presenting it myself, and by the assistance of Mr. Perthieur, the interpreter, in whom we ever found a compassionate friend, we got some small relief. About the first of November I was taken violently ill of a fever, and was carried to the hospital, with my daughter Captive. After a month's residence there, with tolerable good attendance, I recovered from my illness, and went back to my husband. While at the hospital, I found an opportunity to convey the unwelcome tidings of our deplorable situation to my sister, at Montreal, charging her to give my best love to my daughter Susanna, and to inform our fellow prisoners, Labarree and Farnsworth, that our good wishes awaited them. Not a word had we yet heard from poor Sylvanus.

Winter now began to approach, and the severe frosts of Canada operated keenly upon our feelings. Our prison was a horrid defence from the blasts of December; with two chairs and a heap of straw, and two lousy blankets, we may well be supposed to live uncomfortably: but in addition to this, we had but one poor fire a day, and the iron grates gave free access to the chills of the inclement sky. A quart bason was the only thing allowed us to cook our small piece of meat and dirty crusts in, and it must serve at the same time for table furniture. In this sad plight—a prisoner—in jail—winter approaching—conceive reader, for I cannot speak our distress.

Our former benevolent friends, Captain Stowbrow and Vambram, had the peculiar misfortune to be cast into a prison opposite to us. Suspicion of having corresponded with their countrymen, was the crime with which they were charged. Their misfortune did not preclude the exertion of generosity; they frequently sent us, by the waiting maid, bottles of wine, and articles of provision. But the malice of Frenchmen had now arrived to such a pitch, against all our country, that we must be deprived of these comforts. These good men were forbidden their offices of kindness, and our intercourse was entirely prohibited. We however found means, by a stratagem, to effect in some measure, what could not be done by open dealing. When the servants were carrying in our daily supplies, we slipped into the entry, and deposited our letters in an ash box, which were taken by our friends, they leaving one at the same time for us; this served, in some measure, to amuse a dull hour —sometimes we diverted ourselves by the use of Spanish cards; as Mr. Johnson was ignorant of the game, I derived no inconsiderable pleasure from instructing him. But the vigilance of our keepers increased, and our paper and ink were withheld.—We had now been prisoners seventeen months, and our prospects were changing from bad to worse; five months had elapsed since our confinement in this horrid receptacle, except the time we lingered in the hospital. Our jailer was a true descendant from Pharaoh; but, urged by impatience and despair, I softened him so much as to get him to ask Mr. Perthieur to call on us. When the good man came, we described our situation in all the moving terms which our feelings inspired, which in addition to what he saw, convinced him of the reality of our distress. He proposed asking an influential friend of his to call on us, who, perhaps, would devise some mode for our relief. The next day the gentleman came to see us; he was one of those good souls who ever feel for others' woes. He was highly affronted with his countrymen for reducing us to such distress, and declared that the Lord Intendant himself should call on us, and see the extremities to which he had reduced us; he sent, from his own house, that night, a kettle, some candles, and each of us a change of linen.

The next day, January 8th, 1756, Mr. Intendant came to see us; he exculpated himself by saying that we were put there by the special order of Mons. Vaudrieul, the Governor in chief, and that he had no authority to release us. But he would convey a letter from Mr. Johnson to Monsieur, which might have the desired effect. The letter was accordingly written, stating our troubles, and beseeching relief; likewise praying that our son might be got from the Indians and sent to us, with our daughter and sister from Montreal.—

The Gov. returned the following obliging letter:

I have received, Sir, your letter, and am much concerned for the situation you are in. I write to Mr. Longieul, to put you and your wife in the civil jail. Mr. L. Intendant will be so good as to take some notice of the things you stand in need of, and to help you. As to your boy, who is in the hands of the Indians, I will do all that is in my power to get him, but I do not hope to have a good success in it; your child in town, and your sister-in-law are well. If it is some opportunity of doing you some pleasure, I will make use of it, unless some reason might happen that hinder and stop the effects of my good will. If you had not before given some cause of being suspected, you should be at liberty. I am, Sir, your most humble servant,

VAUDRIEUL.

From the receipt of this letter we dated our escape from direful bondage. Mr. Intendant ordered us directly to the new jail, called the civil prison, where our accommodations were infinitely better. We had a decent bed, candles, fuel, and all the conveniences belonging to prisoners of war. Mr. Johnson was allowed fifteen pence per day, on account of a

lieutenant's commission which he held under
George the Second, and I was permitted to
go once a week into the city to purchase
necessaries; and a washerwoman was provided for my use. We were not confined to
the narrow limits of a single room, but were
restrained only by the bounds of the jail yard.
Our situation formed such a contrast with
what we endured in the gloomy criminal
jail, that we imagined ourselves the favorites
of fortune, and in high life.

CHAP. VIII.

*Residence in the Civil Jail, and occurrences
till the twentieth of July,* 1757.

TO be indolent from necessity, has ever
been deemed a formidable evil. No better
witnesses than ourselves can testify the truth
of the remark, although our lodgings were
now such as we envied a month before; yet
to be compelled to continual idleness, was
grievous to be borne. We derived some
amusement from the cultivation of a small
garden, within the jail yard; but a continued
sameness of friends and action, rendered our
time extremely wearisome.

About a month after our arrival at this new
abode, one Captain Milton, with his crew,
who, with their vessel, were taken at sea,
were brought prisoners of war to the same
place. Milton was lodged in our apartment;
he had all the rude boisterous airs of a seaman,
without the least trait of a gentleman, which
rendered him a very troublesome companion.
His impudence was consummate, but that was
not the greatest evil; while some new recruits
were parading before the prison one day, Milton addressed them in very improper language
from our window, which was noticed directly
by city authority, who, supposing it to be Mr.

Johnson, ordered him into the dungeon.
Deeply affected by this new trouble, I again
called on my friend Mr. Perthieur, who, after
having ascertained the facts, got him released.
Mr. Milton was then put into other quarters.

A new jailer, who had an agreeable lady for
his wife, now made our situation still more
happy. My little daughters played with hers,
and learned the French language. But my
children were some trouble—the eldest, Polly,
could slip out into the street under the gate
and often came nigh being lost: I applied to
the centinel, and he kept her within proper
bounds.

Capt. M'Neil and his brother, from Boston,
were brought to us as prisoners; they informed us of the state of politics in our own
country, and told us some interesting news
about some of our friends at home.

In the morning of the 13th of August, our
jailer, with moon-eyes, came to congratulate
us on the taking of Oswego by the French.
We entered little into his spirit of joy, prefer-
ring much to hear good news from the other
side. We were soon visited by some of the
prisoners, who had surrendered. Col. Schuyler was in the number, who, with the gentlemen in his suit, made us a generous present.

The remainder of the summer and fall, of
1756, passed off without any sensible varia-
tion. We frequently heard from Montreal;

my sister was very well situated, in the family
of the Lieut. Governor, and my eldest daughter was caressed by her three mothers. Could
I have heard from my son, half my trouble
would have ended.

In December I was delivered of a son,
which lived but a few hours, and was buried
under the Cathedral Church.

In the winter I received a letter from my
sister, containing the sad tidings of my father's
death. He was killed the 16th of June, 1756,
about fifty rods east from the main street in
Charlestown, on the same lot on which my
youngest brother now lives. My father and
my brother, Moses Willard, were repairing
some fence on the rear of the lots, and the
Indians, being secreted in the bushes a small
distance from them, fired upon them, and shot
my father dead on the spot. They then sprang
to catch my brother—he ran for the fort, and
there being a rise of ground to pass towards
the fort, the Indian that followed him, finding
that he could not catch him, sent his spear
which pierced his thigh, with which he ran to
the fort. He is now living in Charlestown,
and still carries the scar occasioned by the
wound.

The melancholy tidings of the death of my
father, in addition to my other afflictions, wore
upon me sensibly; and too much grief reduced me to a weak condition. I was taken

sick, and carried to the hospital, where, after a month's lingering illness, I found myself able to return.

The commencement of the year 1757 passed off without a prospect of liberty. Part of our fellow prisoners were sent to France, but we made no voyage out of the jail yard. About the first of May, we petitioned Mons. Vaudrieul to permit our sister to come to us. Our prayer was granted, and in May we had the pleasure of seeing her, after an absence of two years. She had supported herself by her needle, in the family of the Lieut. Governor, where she was treated extremely well, and received a present of four crowns, at parting.

Impatient of confinement, we now made another attempt to gain our liberty. Mr. Perthieur conducted us to the house of the Lord Intendant, to whom we petitioned in pressing terms; stating, that we had now been prisoners almost three years, and had suffered every thing but death, and that would be our speedy portion unless we had relief. His Lordship listened with seeming pity, and promised to lay our case before the head man, at Montreal, and give us an answer, in seven days; at the expiration of which time, we had a permit to leave the prison. It is not easy to describe the effect of such news; those only, who have felt the horrors of confinement, can figure to themselves the happiness we enjoyed, when breathing, once more, the air of liberty. We took lodgings in town, where we tarried till the first of June; when a cartel ship arrived to carry prisoners to England for an exchange. Mr. Johnson wrote an urgent letter to Mons. Vaudrieul, praying that his family might be included with those who were to take passage. Monsieur wrote a very encouraging letter back, promising that he and his family should sail; and that his daughter, Susanna, should be sent to him— he concluded by congratulating him on his good prospects, and ordering the Governor of Quebec to afford us his assistance. This letter was dated June the 27th.

That the reader may the better realize our situation and feelings on this occasion, the copies of the letters are here inserted:

SIR—A report being current in town that all the English prisoners were exchanged and are to be sent off soon, made me apply to Mr. Perthieur to know of him whether I was included. He told me that he knew nothing of the affair; this makes me take the liberty to apply to your Excellency, to pray you to have compassion on my distressed situation, and to send me away with others. It is now almost three years that I have been a prisoner with my family, which has already reduced me to extreme want, and, unless your Excellency pities me, I am likely to continue miserable forever. Were I all alone, the affair would not be so melancholy—but having a wife, and sister, and four children, involved in my misfortune, makes it the more deplorable. And to add to all my misery, my boy is still in the hands of the savages, notwithstanding I rely upon the letter your Excellency did me the honor to condescend to write me, to assure me of your endeavors in withdrawing him out of their hands—and I must therefore once more take the liberty to entreat you to do it, and send him down here, as well as my girl, still at Montreal, and their ransom shall be immediately paid.

As I have your Excellency's parole to be one of the first prisoners sent away, I will not give myself leave to doubt, or fear that I shall not—and your Excellency well knows that your predecessor, Mr. D'Longueille, gave me his, that upon returning from New-England with the ransom of myself and family, I should be at liberty; nevertheless I was not, owing to want of opportunity.

Your Excellency made me the same promise, and the occasion now presenting itself, I well know that I have only to put you in mind of it in order to the gaining of my desire.

Should it be impossible to get my children with me, (though that would be the greatest of misfortunes) yet that should not hinder me from going myself, in expectation of *peace,* when I might once more return and fetch them myself.

I hope your Excellency will easily forgive the trouble my miserable situation obliges me to give you, and that you will, with your wonted goodness, grant my request.

I am, with profound esteem,
Sir, your most humble, and
most obedient servant,
JAMES JOHNSON.

Mons. D'Vaudrieul.
Quebec, 21st June, 1757.

Answer to the foregoing.

TRANSLATION.

Montreal, June 27, 1757.

SIR—I have received your letter of the current month. I will consent, with pleasure, to your being sent back to England in the packet-boat, which I am about to dispatch, with some English prisoners. For this purpose, I will send your daughter to Quebec by the first vessel. I am glad to learn, that you are in a situation to pay her ransom. I wish that you might find the same facility, on the part of the savages, to get your son out of their hands. When I shall have dispatched your daughter, I will write to Mons. D'Longueil to send you back, with your family, after you shall have satisfied the persons, who

have made advances for their recovery from the savages. I am, Sir, your affectionate servant,   VAUDRIEUL.
Mr. James Johnson.

This tide of good fortune almost wiped away the remembrance of three years adversity. We began our preparations for embarkation with alacrity. Mr. Johnson wrote St. Luc Lucorne, for the seven hundred livres, due on Mr. Cuyler's order, but his request was, and still is, unsatisfied. This was a period big with every thing propitious and happy. The idea of leaving a country where I had suffered the keenest distress, during two months and a half with the savages—been bowed down by every mortification and insult, which could arise from the misfortunes of my husband, in New-England; and where I had spent two years in sickness and despair, in a prison too shocking to mention, contributed to fill the moment with all the happiness, which the benevolent reader will conceive my due, after sufferings so intense; to consummate the whole, my daughter was to be returned to my arms, who had been absent more than two years. There was a good prospect of our son's being released from the Indians; the whole formed such a lucky combination of fortunate events, that the danger of twice crossing the ocean to gain our native shore, vanished in a moment. My family were all in the same joyful mood, and hailed the happy day when we should sail for England.

But little did we think that this sunshine of prosperity was so soon to be darkened by the heaviest clouds of misfortune.

I am not in the habit of placing much dependence on dreams, but the one I shall now relate, has been so completely followed, in the course of my great misfortune, I have thought proper to insert it, for the further amusement, if not the satisfaction, of the reader. I tho't our friend, Mr. Perthieur, came with a paper in his hand, and delivered it to me. On opening the paper, I found two rings, the one a very beautiful gold dress ring, the other a mourning ring, which were presents sent, as he said, to me. In putting the dress ring on my finger I broke it into many pieces, and it fell down, and I could not find the pieces again. The mourning ring I kept whole, and put it on my finger. But when I awoke, behold, it was a dream. I informed my husband of it in the morning, and said to him, I much fear some further misfortune will happen to us. While I was in the civil jail this dream occurred, and whether it was a prelude to what follows, the reader will judge for himself.

Three days before the appointed hour for

sailing, the ship came down from Montreal, without my daughter; in a few moments I met Mr. Perthieur, who told me that counter orders had come, and Mr. Johnson must be retained a prisoner; only my two little daughters, sister and myself could go. This was calamity indeed; to attempt such a long wearisome voyage, without money and without acquaintance, and to leave a husband and two children in the hands of enemies, was too abhorrent for reflection. But it was an affair of importance, and required weighty consideration. Accordingly the next day a solemn council of all the prisoners in the city was held at the coffee-house.—Col. Schuyler was president, and after numerous arguments for and against were heard, it was voted, by a large majority, that I should go—I, with hesitation, gave my consent. Some, perhaps, will censure the measure as rash, and others may applaud my courage; but I had so long been accustomed to danger and distress, in the most menacing forms they could assume, that I was now almost insensible to their threats; and this act was not a little biassed by desperation. Life could no longer retain its value, if lingered out in the inimical regions of Canada. In Europe I should at least find friends, if not acquaintance; and among the numerous vessels bound to America I might chance to get a passage. But then,

to leave a tender husband, who had so long,
at the hazard of his life, preserved my own;
to part, perhaps forever, from two children
put all my resolution to the test, and shook
my boasted firmness.

Col. Schuyler, whom we ever found our
benevolent friend, promised to use his influence for Mr. Johnson's release, and for the
redemption of our children.

On the 20th of July, we went on board the
vessel, accompanied by Mr. Johnson, who
went with us to take leave. We were introduced to the Captain, who was a gentleman,
and a person of great civility; he shewed us
the best cabin, which was to be the place of
our residence, & after promising my husband
that the voyage should be made as agreeable
to me as possible, he gave orders for weighing
anchor. The time was now come that we
must part—Mr. Johnson took me by the
hand—our tears imposed silence—I saw him
step into the barge; but my two little children, sister and myself were bound for Europe.

We fell down the river St. Lawrence but a
small distance that night. The next morning,
the Captain, with a cheerful countenance,
came to our cabin, and invited us to rise and
take our leave of Quebec; none but myself
complied, and I gazed, as long as sight would
permit, at the place where I had left my
dearest friend.

CHAP. IX.

Voyage to Plymouth.—Occurrences.—Sailing from Plymouth to Portsmouth, from thence by the way of Cork to New York.

All my fears and affliction did not prevent my feeling some little joy at being released from the jurisdiction of Frenchmen. I could pardon the Indians, for their vindictive spirit, because they had no claim to the benefits of civilization. But the French, who give lessons of politeness, to the rest of the world, can derive no advantage from the plea of ignorance. The blind superstition which is inculcated by their monks and friars, doubtless stifles, in some measure, the exertion of pity towards their enemies; and the common herd, which includes almost seven eighths of their number, have no advantages from education. To these sources I attribute most of my sufferings. But I found some benevolent friends, whose generosity I shall ever recollect with the warmest gratitude.

The commencement of the voyage had every favorable presage; the weather was fine, the sailors cheerful, and the ship in good trim. My accommodations in the Captain's family were very commodious; a boy was allowed me, for my particular use. We sailed with excellent fortune till the 19th of August, when we hove in sight of old Plymouth, and at 4 o'clock in the afternoon dropped anchor.

The next day all but myself and family were taken from the vessel; we felt great anxiety at being left, and began to fear that fortune was not willing to smile on us, even on these shores; we waited in despair thirty or forty hours, and found no relief. The Captain observing our despondency, began his airs of gaiety to cheer us; he assured us that we should not suffer—that if the English would not receive us, he would take us to France and make us happy. But at last an officer came on board, to see if the vessel was prepared for the reception of French prisoners. We related to him our situation; he conducted us on shore, and applied to the Admiral for directions—who ordered us lodgings and the King's allowance of two shillings sterling per day, for our support. Fortunately we were lodged in a house where resided Captain John Tufton Mason, whose name will be familiar to the inhabitants of New-Hampshire, on account of his patent. He very kindly interested himself in our favour, and wrote to Messrs. Thomlinson and Apthorp, agents at London for the Province of New-Hampshire, soliciting their assistance in my behalf. We tarried at Plymouth but a fortnight, during which time I received much attention, and had to gratify many inquisitive friends with the history of my sufferings.

There was one little circumstance that took place while we were at Plymouth, which, perhaps, will be pleasing to some of my young readers. My little daughter, Captive, had completely acquired the French tongue, so as to be very pert and talkative in it, but she could not speak a word of English. She had been accustomed, at Quebec, to go to market, or anywhere among the shops, just as she pleased, to buy biscuit, gingerbread, or any such thing that she wanted; and although she used to carry her money to pay for whatever she bought, yet she generally brought it back again, and sometimes more with it. Of course, she grew very bold; for as she knew nothing of danger, so she feared nothing; and although the sentinels would sometimes use very rough language to her, and threaten to run her thro' with the bayonet, yet she could return the same language to them, and as they never had hurt her, so she did not believe they ever would; and, being lawless, she went where she had a mind to. Polly, remembering the English tongue, never obtained the French so as to speak it fluently. After we had taken lodgings at Plymouth, Captive appeared to be very much put out because she could not make the English understand her; nor could she any better

understand them; and she imputed it alto-
gether to their ignorance and impertinence.
The lady of the house gave Polly a biscuit,
which being observed by Captive, she wanted
one also. Polly offered her part of hers, but
she would not touch it, she wanted a whole
one, but could not make her want known.
The lady offered her other things, which only
vexed her. Being very much fatigued and
unwell, I had laid down in my chamber, in
order to get some rest, when my little Captive
came up to me with this bitter complaint, and
said the lady was the most *impertinent* woman
she ever saw. She had given Polly a biscuit
and had not given her any, and when she
asked her for one she would offer her something else. Why, my dear, said I, you are a
little French girl, and these are English
people; the lady did not understand you;
they do not talk here as they do in Quebec.
But Captive was very much vexed, and had
much to say, which I think not proper to
recite, and finally concluded by saying she
would go to market and buy some biscuit
for herself. Why, my child, continued I, you
cannot find the market here, you will get lost,
or the market women will take you and carry
you off and sell you, and I shall never see you
again. And with this conversation I pacified
her, as I supposed, and fell asleep. When I
awoke, not observing her immediately, I

enquired, "Where is my Captive?" I do not
know, said Polly, she came down stairs a little
while ago, and said she would go to market,
but I told her she must not, and I have not
seen her since. "The Lord have mercy,"
said I, "she is gone, and she will be lost, if she
is not saught after immediately." On enquiry
of a market woman, she said she had seen a
little girl, in a very singular dress, such an one
as she had never seen before, almost half a
mile off; she spoke to her, but she gave her
no answer. I immediately sent a servant after
her. She was completely dressed in the
French fashion, which attracted the notice of
every one that saw her. The servant found
her returning home. She had got her *mau-
shum* which is a little sack or bag hanging
from the left shoulder, full of biscuit, and
appeared to be very happy until the servant
met her. But her joy was soon turned into
sorrow! The servant attempted to carry her;
and she, thinking it was somebody that had
come to carry her off, as I told her they would,
screamed, scratched and bit, till his face was
besmeared with blood, and he was glad to
put her down. Then she ran to get away
from him, and fell down in the streets till her
clothes were all besmeared with mud and
water. But he kept watch of her, and headed
her when he found she was going wrong, until
he got her back. And in a sad plight they

appeared; she was covered with mud and water, (as it had lately rained, and she had fallen several times in the gutters of the streets) and he was besmeared with blood. But after she got over her fright so as to give a history of her adventure, it was amusing indeed. She waited till she found I was asleep, when she crept slyly to the bed, and took some coppers out of my pocket that hung by the head of my bed, and off she started. She went into a number of shops, but she saw no biscuit, neither could she understand a word that any of them said. But she concluded they were all impertinent creatures, and so passed on; till at length she came to a house where she saw the door was open and the ladies were drinking tea. She went in, and saw biscuit, which was the thing she was after, on the table. She threw down her money upon the table and took her hand, full of biscuit, and went out. The ladies followed her, and came out gabbling round her, *blub, lub, lub, lub,* but she could not tell a word they said. They however filled her bag with biscuit, which was all that she wanted, and she set out for home, feeling as happy as any little creature could well be, until she met the servant before mentioned.

But if the reader has been sufficiently amused with little history, he will now be kind enough to proceed with me in my narrative.

Capt. Mason procured me a passage to Portsmouth, in the Rainbow man of war, from whence I was to take passage in a packet for America. Just as I stepped on board the Rainbow, a good lady, with her son, came to make me a visit; her curiosity to see a person of my description was not abated by my being on my passage; she said she could not sleep till she had seen the person who had suffered such hard fortune. After she had asked all the questions that time would allow of, she gave me a guinea, and half a guinea to my sister, and a muslin handkerchief to each of our little girls. On our arrival at Portsmouth, the packet had sailed; the Captain of the Rainbow, not finding it convenient to keep us with him, introduced us on board the Royal Ann.

Wherever we lived, we found the best friends and the politest treatment.—It will be thought singular, that a defenceless woman should suffer so many changes, without meeting some insults and many incivilities. But during my long residence on board the various vessels, I received the must delicate attention from my companions. The officers were assiduous in making my situation agreeable, and readily proffered their services.

While on board the Royal Ann, I received the following letters; the reader will excuse the recitation; it would be ingratitude not to record such conspicuous acts of benevolence.

Plymouth, Sept. 13, 1757.

MADAM,

Late last post night I received an answer from Mr. Apthorp, who is partner with Mr. Thomlinson, the agent for New-Hampshire, with a letter enclosed to you, which gave you liberty to draw on him for fifteen guineas. As Madam Hornech was just closing her letter to you, I gave it her, to enclose for you; I now write again to London on your behalf. You must immediately write Mr. Apthorp, what you intend to do, and what further you would have him and our friends at London do for you.

I hope you have received the benefaction of the charitable ladies in this town. All friends here commiserate your misfortunes, and wish you well, together with your sister and children.

Your friend and countryman to serve.

JOHN T. MASON.

MRS. JOHNSON.

London, Sept. 7, 1757.

MADAM,

I received a letter from Capt. Mason, dated the thirtieth of last month, giving an account of your unfortunate situation, and yesterday Mr. Thomlinson, who is ill in the country, sent me your letter, together with Capt. Mason's to him, with the papers relative to you. In consequence of which, I this day applied to a number of gentlemen in your behalf, who very readily gave their assistance; but as I am a stranger to the steps you intend to pursue, I can only give you liberty, at present, to draw on me for ten or fifteen guineas, for which sum your bill shall be paid, and when you furnish me with information, I shall very cheerfully give any furtherance in my power, to your relief, when I shall also send you a list of your benefactors.

I am, Madam,

Your most humble servant,

JOHN APTHORP.

MRS. SUSANNAH JOHNSON.

LETTER FROM H. GROVE.

I have now the pleasure to let dear Mrs. Johnson know the goodness of Mrs. Hornech; she has collected seven pounds for you, and sent it to Mrs. Brett, who lives in the yard at Portsmouth, to beg her favours to you, in any thing she can do to help or assist you. She is a good lady; do go to her, and let her know your distress. Capt. Mason has got a letter this post, but he is not at home; cannot tell you further. You will excuse this scrawl, likewise my not enlarging—as Mr. Hornech waits to send it away. Only believe me, madam, you have my earnest prayers to God, to help and assist you. My mama's compli-

ments with mine, and begs to wait on you,
and believe me, dear Mrs. Johnson, yours in
all events to serve you.

HANNAH GROVE.

Sunday Eve, 10 *o'clock.*

I received the donation, and Mr. Apthorp
sent me the fifteen guineas. I sincerely
lament that he omitted sending me the names
of my benefactors.

The Captain of the Royal Ann, supposing
my situation with him, might not be so convenient, applied to the mayor, for a permit
for me to take lodgings in the city, which was
granted. I took new lodgings, where I tarried
three or four days when orders came for me
to be on board the Orange man of war, in
three hours, which was to sail for America.
We made all possible dispatch, but when we
got to the shore, we were astonished to find
the ship too far under way to be overtaken.
No time was to be lost, I applied to a water-
man, to carry us to a merchantman, who was
weighing anchor at a distance, to go in the
same fleet. He hesitated long enough to pro-
nounce a chapter of oaths, and rowed us off.
When we came to the vessel, I petitioned the
Captain to take us on board, till he overtook
the Orange. He directly flew into a violent
passion, and offered greater insults than I had
ever received during my whole voyage; he

swore we were women of bad fame, who wished to follow the army, and that he would have nothing to do with us. I begged him to calm his rage, and we would convince him of his error. But, fortunately, the victualler of the fleet happened to be in the ship who at this moment stepped forward with his roll of names, and told the outrageous Captain that he would soon convince him, whether we deserved notice, by searching his list. He soon found our names, and the Captain began to beg pardon. He took us on board, and apologized for his rudeness. We sailed with a fair wind for Cork, where the fleet took provision. We tarried a fortnight in this place, during which time the Captain of the Orange came on board to see me, and to offer me a birth in his vessel; but that being a battle ship, it was thought best for me to stay where I then was. After weighing anchor at Cork, we had a passage of seven weeks, remarkably pleasant, to New-York. On the tenth of December we dropped anchor at Sandy Hook; on the eleventh, I had the supreme felicity to find myself on shore in my native country, after an absence of three years, three months, and eleven days.

CHAP. X.

The History ends.

I MIGHT descant for many a page on the felicity I felt on being once more in my own country; but others can guess my feelings better than I can tell them. The Mayor of New-York ordered lodgings for us; here I had the pleasure of meeting my friend, Col. Schuyler, who gave me much information about affairs in Canada; he told me that my husband had been released, and taken passage in a cartel ship for Halifax, and that he had redeemed my son from the Indians, for the sum of five hundred livres.

My fellow prisoner, Labarree, had made his escape from the French, and had been in New-York a few days before, on his way home.

The reader may reasonably suppose that a more than ordinary friendship might subsist between us on account of his preserving the life of my infant, and rendering every assistance, which it was in his power to perform for us, on our journey through the wilderness. Mr. Labarree resided in Charlestown about two miles from where I lived. We often visited each other after our return, and frequently amused ourselves in the recollection of our journey with the Indians. He amused himself much with my daughter Captive, in her childhood, and was always that benevolent friend through life, which was so peculiarly manifested on the day and journey of our captivity. It so happened that my daughter was in Charlestown at the time of his last sickness and death. She visited him and tarried several days; and attended him but only a few days before his death. He often mentioned with satisfaction the peculiar situation of our captivity: little, he said, did he think that he was preserving the life of her in his arms, (speaking of my daughter) who should be one to attend him in his last days; but that he was happy to have her with him, for she ever appeared to him almost as near as one of his own children. Mr. Labarree was one of those good men who feel for the misfortunes of others. He died August 3d, 1803, aged 79 years.

We tarried in New-York ten days—then took water passage for New-Haven, where I had the good fortune to find a number of officers, who had been stationed at Charlestown the preceding summer, who gratified my curiosity with intelligence respecting my relations and friends in that place. Some of these gentlemen, among whom was Col. Whiting, kindly undertook to assist us on our journey home, by the way of Springfield. At

Hartford we found some gentlemen who were bound for Charlestown; they solicited my sister* to go in company with them, to which she assented.

When within half a dozen miles of Springfield, Mr. Ely, a benevolent friend of Mr. Johnson's, sent his two sons, with a sleigh to convey me to his house, where I proposed staying till some of my friends could hear of my arrival. Fortunately, Mr. Johnson about the same time arrived at Boston, but misfortune had not yet filled the measure of his calamity. He had no sooner landed, than he was put under guard, on suspicion of not performing his duty in the redemption of the Canada prisoners, which suspicion was occasioned by his remissness in producing his vouchers. But the following certificate procured his liberty:

This is to certify, whom it may concern, that the bearer, Lieutenant James Johnson, inhabitant in the town of Charlestown, in the Province of New-Hampshire, in New-England; who, together with his family, were taken by the Indians on the 30th of August 1754, has ever since continued a steady and faithful subject to his Majesty King George, and has used his utmost endeavors to redeem

*Miss Miriam Willard was afterwards married to the Rev. Mr. Whitney, of Shirley, Massachusetts.

his own family, and all others belonging to the Province aforesaid, that were in the hands of the French and Indian, which he cannot yet accomplish; and that both himself and family have undergone innumerable hardships and affliction since they have been prisoners in Canada.

In testimony of which, we the subscribers, officers in his Britannic Majesty's service, and now prisoners of war at Quebec, have thought it necessary to grant him this certificate, and do recommend him as an object worthy the aid and compassion of every honest Englishman.

Signed

PETER SCHUYLER,
ANDREW WATKINS,
WILLIAM MARTIN,
WILLIAM PADGETT.

Quebec, Sept. 16, 1757.

To compensate him for this misfortune, Gov. Pownal recommended a grant, which the General Court complied with, and gave him one hundred dollars from the treasury, and he was recorded a faithful subject of King George.

After his dismission from the guards in Boston, he proceeded directly for Charlestown. When within fifteen miles of Springfield, he was met by a gentleman who had just before seen me, who gave him the best news he could have heard; although it was then late at night, he lost not a moment. At two o'clock in the morning of the first of January 1758, I again embraced my dearest friend—happy new year, with pleasure would I describe my emotions of joy, could language paint them sufficiently forcible; but the feeble pen shrinks from the task.

Charlestown was still a frontier town, and suffered from savage depredations, which rendered it an improper residence for me; consequently I went to Lancaster.

Mr. Johnson, in a few days, set out for New-York, to adjust his Canada accounts. But on his journey he was persuaded by Gov. Pownal to take a Captain's commission,* and

---

*This commission was dated at Boston the 30th day of March, in the 31st year of the reign of his Majesty, King George the Second, A. D. 1758, and commissioned him to be a Captain of a company in the battalion of light infantry to be formed out of the forces then raised by the Governor for a general invasion of Canada, commanded by Colonel Oliver Pattridge.

When he arrived at Fort Edward, three companies were selected under the immediate care and command of Maj. Hawks, and Capt. Johnson was one of them. There were many there of the soldiers who were acquainted with Capt. Johnson, and desired to be enrolled in his company, which was complied with. Deacon Thomas Putnam, now of Charlestown, engaged in his company as a serjeant, and marched on with him to Ticonderoga—was with him when the battle began in which Capt. Johnson was killed, and gives the following account of the same:

join the forces bound for Ticonderoga: where he was killed on the 8th of July following, in the battle that proved fatal to Lord How, while fighting for his country. Humanity will weep with me. The cup of sorrow was now replete with bitter drops. All my former miseries were lost in the affliction of a widow.

In October, 1758, I was informed that my son Sylvanus was at Northampton, sick of a scald. I hastened to the place, and found him in a deplorable situation; he was brought there by Major Putnam, afterwards Gen. Putnam, with Mrs. How and her family, who had returned from captivity. The town of

---

"On the 8th of July, 1748, Captain Johnson's company was ordered on the left wing of the army; and we arrived within gun-shot of the breastwork, when the enemy fired upon us. We in turn fired at them, whenever we had a chance to get sight at their heads, above the breastwork, till we had discharged a dozen or more shots, at which time the firing appeared to cease on the part of the enemy. Immediately the enemy hoisted a flag which was supposed by Capt. Johnson and others to be a signal that they were about to give up to our army. A part of his company being still at some distance to the left, Capt. Johnson ordered me to go immediately to the left to have those cease firing, saying with joy, "the day (or battle) is ours." I immediately set out, climbing over brush, trees and logs, laying 8 or 10 feet from the ground. When stepping on a tree, some rods distance from where I left Capt. Johnson, there was a full volley fired from the enemy. I escaped from being wounded, a ball only grazing

Northampton had taken the charge of him—his situation was miserable; when I found him he had no recollection of me, but after some conversation, he had some confused ideas of me, but no remembrance of his father. It was four years since I had seen him, he was then eleven years old; during his absence he had entirely forgotten the English language, spoke a little broken French, but was perfect in Indian. He had been with the savages three years, and one year with the French; but his habits were somewhat Indian: he had been with them in their hunting excursions, and suffered numerous hardships—he could

---

my hat. I let myself down as soon as I could, and made the best way possible to escape their fire. I soon found some of my companions that were with Capt. Johnson, who gave me the melancholy tidings of his being shot through the head, and expired instantly on the spot where I left him. His body was left on the ground, but his arms and equipage, together with some of his clothing, were brought off. I was acquainted with him from my youth—knew him in the former war, when a Lieut. under the command of Edward Hartwell, Esq. posted at Lunenburg, Townsend and Narraganset No. 2, &c. He was universally beloved by his company, and equally lamented at his death. He was the *soldier's friend*, and a friend to his country—was of easy manners, pleasant, good humored, yet strict to obey his orders and see that those under his command did the same. The loss to his wife and family was irreparable—his acquaintance also lost an agreeable companion, a valuable member of society, as well as a faithful and valiant soldier."

brandish a tomahawk or bend the bow, but these habits wore off by degrees. I carried him from that place to Lancaster, where he lived a few years with Col. Aaron Willard.

I lived in Lancaster till October 1759, when I returned to old Charlestown.—The sight of my former residence afforded a strange mixture of joy and grief, while the desolations of war, and the loss of a number of dear and valuable friends, combined to give the place an air of melancholy. Soon after my arrival, Major Rogers returned from an expedition against the village St. Francis, which he had destroyed and killed most of the inhabitants. He brought with him a young Indian prisoner, who stopped at my house, the moment he saw me he cried, my God, my God, here is my sister; it was my little brother Sabatis, who formerly used to bring the cows for me, when I lived at my Indian masters. He was transported to see me, and declared that he was still my brother, and I must be his sister. Poor fellow! The fortune of war had left him without a single relation, but with his country's enemies, he could find one who too sensibly felt his miseries; I felt the purest pleasure in administering to his comfort.

I was extremely fortunate in receiving by one of Major Rogers's men, a bundle of Mr. Johnson's papers, which he found in pillaging St. Francis. The Indians took them

when we were captivated, and they had lain
at St. Francis five years.

Sabatis went from Charlestown to Crown
Point with Major Rogers. When he got to
Otter Creek, he met my son Sylvanus, who
was in the army with Col. Willard: he recog-
nized him, and clasping him in his arms,
"My God," says he, "the fortune of war!"—
I shall ever remember this young Indian with
affection; he had a high sense of honor and
good behaviour, he was affable, good natured
and polite.

My daughter Susannah was still in Canada
—but as I had the fullest assurances that
every attention was paid to her education and
welfare by her three mothers, I felt less
anxiety that I otherwise might have done.

Every one will imagine that I have paid
affliction her utmost demand, the pains of
imprisonment, the separation from my children, the keen sorrow occasioned by the death
of a butchered father, and the severe grief
arising from my husband's death, will amount
to a sum, perhaps, unequalled. But still my
family must be doomed to further and severe
persecutions, from the savages. In the commencement of the summer of 1760, my
brother in law, Mr. Joseph Willard, son of
the Rev. Mr. Willard of Rutland, who was
killed by the Indians in Lovell's war, with his
wife and five children, who lived but two

miles distant from me, were taken by a party of Indians. They were carried much the same rout that I was to Montreal. Their journey of fourteen days through the wilderness, was a series of miseries, unknown to any but those who have suffered Indian captivity; they lost two children, whose deaths were owing to savage barbarity. The history of their captivity would almost equal my own, but the reader's commiseration and pity must now be exhausted. No more of anguish, no more of sufferings.

They arrived at Montreal a few days before the French surrendered it to the English; and after four months' absence, returned home, and brought my daughter Susanna to my arms; while I rejoiced at again meeting my child, whom I had not seen for above five years, I felt extremely grateful to the Mrs. Jaissons, for the affectionate attention they had bestowed on her. As they had received her as their child, they had made their affluent fortune subservient to her best interest. To give her the accomplishments of a polite education had been their principal care, she had contracted an ardent love for them, which never will be obliterated. Their parting was an affectionate scene of tears. They never forgot her during their lives; she has eight letters from them, which are proofs of the warmest friendship. My daughter did not know me at her return, and spoke nothing but French; my son spoke Indian, so that my family was a mixture of nations.

Mr. Farnsworth, my only fellow prisoner whose return I have not mentioned, came home a little before.

Thus, by the goodness of Providence, we all returned in the course of six painful years to the place from whence we were taken. The long period of our captivity, and the severity of our sufferings, will be called uncommon and unprecedented. But we even found some friends to pity, among our most persecuting enemies; and from the various shapes in which mankind appeared, we learned many valuable lessons. Whether in the wilds of Canada, the horrid jails of Quebec, or in our voyage to Europe, daily occurrences happened to convince us that the passions of men are as various as their complexions. And altho' my sufferings were often increased by the selfishness of this world's spirit, yet the numerous testimonies of generosity I received, bids me suppress the charge of neglect, or want of benevolence. That I have been an unfortunate woman, all will grant;—yet my misfortunes, while they enriched my experience, and taught me the value of patience, have increased my gratitude to the Author of all blessings, whose goodness and mercy have preserved my life to the present time.

During the time of my widowhood, misfortune and disappointment were my intimate companions. In the settlement of my husband's estate, the delay and perplexity was distressing. I made three journeys to Portsmouth, fourteen to Boston, and three to Springfield, to effect the settlement. Whether my captivity had taught me to be ungrateful, or whether imagination formed a catalogue of evils, I will not pretend to say; but from the year 1754 to the present day, greater misfortunes have apparently fallen to my share than to mankind in general, and the meteor happiness has eluded my grasp. The life of a widow is peculiarly afflictive,—but my numerous and long journies over roads imminently bad, and incidents that seemed to baffle all my plans and foresight, render mine more unfortunate than common.

But I found many attentive friends, whose assistance and kindness will always claim my gratitude. Colonel White of Leominster, with whom I had lived from the time I was eight years old until I married, was extremely affectionate and kind—in his house I found a welcome home. Mr. Samuel Ely of Springfield, who was the friend of my husband, rendered me numerous kindnesses. Colonel Murray of Rutland, and Col. Chandler of Worcester, were very friendly and kind. Mr. Clarke, deputy secretary, Gov. Pownall, and

Gov. Wentworth, exerted their influence for me in attempting to procure a grant from the General Assembly.

In one of my journies to Portsmouth, I conversed with Capt. Adams, who was in Europe at the time I was—he informed me that while there, Mr. Apthorp gave him fourteen pounds sterling, for the purpose of conveying me and my family to America: my sailing with the convoy prevented my receiving this kindness.

During the four years of my widowhood I was in quite an unsettled situation; sometimes receiving my children who were returning from captivity, and at others settling the estate of my deceased husband. In October, 1759, I moved to Charlestown, and took possession of my patrimony, consisting of a house which Col. Whiting had generously assisted my mother in building; in copartnership with my brother Moses Willard, I kept a small store, which was of service in supporting my family, and settling my husband's estate. I have received, by petitioning, from the General Assembly of New-Hampshire, forty-two pounds, to indemnify myself and family for losses sustained by our country's enemies. This was of eminent service to me. Mr. Johnson left with Mr. Charles Apthorp, of Boston, the sum which my son's redemption cost, for Col. Schuyler, who had paid the same. But the General Assembly of Massachusetts afterwards paid Col. Schuyler his demand for redeeming my son.

By Mr. Johnson I had seven children; two sons and a daughter died in infancy. Sylvanus, with whom the reader is acquainted, now lives in Charlestown. Susanna married Capt. Samuel Wetherbee, and has been the mother of fifteen children, among which were five at two births. Polly married Col. Timothy Bedel, of Haverhill—died in August 1789. Captive married Col. George Kimball.

In the year 1762 I married Mr. John Hastings; he was one of the first settlers in Charlestown; I recollect to have seen him when I visited the place in the year 1744—he suffered much by the Indians, and assisted in defending the town during the wars. By him I had seven children; one daughter and four sons died in their infancy. Theodosia is married to Mr. Stephen Hasham; Randilla died at the age of twenty-two—she lived from her infancy with Mr. Samuel Taylor of Rockingham, by whom she was treated with great affection. I have had thirty-eight grand-children, and twenty-eight great grand-children. I lived, till within a few years, on the same spot where the Indians took us from in 1754, but the face of nature has so changed that old savage fears are all banished.

I have lived to see good days after so many scenes of sorrow and affliction: I have participated largely in the comforts of life, although the winter of my life has not been rendered so happy as I could have wished.

My whole life has been a strange mixture of good and evil, of pleasure and affliction, and I hope and trust I have profited by the reality, that others may be profited by the history, which I leave as a legacy to my friends, as I am now waiting my departure, when I hope to leave the world in peace. My vacant hours I have often employed in reflecting on the various scenes that have marked the different stages of my life. When viewing the present rising generation, in the bloom of health, and enjoying those gay pleasures which shed their exhilarating influence so plentifully in the morn of life, I look back to my early days, when I too was happy, and basking in the sunshine of good fortune: Little do they think, that the meridian of their lives can possibly be rendered miserable by captivity or a prison; as little too did I think that my gilded prospects could be obscured; but it was the happy delusion of youth, and I fervently wish there was no deception. But that Being, who "sits upon the circle of the earth, and views the inhabitants as grasshoppers," allots our fortunes.

Although I have drank so largely from the cup of sorrow, yet the many happy days I have seen, may be considered as no small compensation. Twice has my country been ravaged by war since my remembrance: I have detailed the share I bore in the first,—in the last, although the place in which I lived was not a field of bloody battle, yet its vicinity to Ticonderoga, and the savages that ravaged the Coos country, rendered it perilous and distressing. But now no one can set a higher value on the smiles of peace, than myself. The savages are driven beyond the lakes, and our country has no enemies. The gloomy wilderness that fifty years ago secreted the Indian and the beast of prey, has vanished away; and the thrifty farm smiles in its stead: the Sundays that were then employed in guarding a fort, are now quietly devoted to worship: the tomahawk and scalping knife have given place to the plough-share and sickle, and prosperous husbandry now thrives, where the terrors of death once chilled us with fear.

My numerous progeny have often gathered around me, to hear the sufferings once felt by their aunt or grandmother, and wonder at their magnitude.

My daughter, Captive, still keeps the dress she appeared in when brought to my bed-side by the French nurse, at the Ticonderoga hospital; and often refreshes my memory with past scenes, when showing it to her children. These things yield a kind of melancholy pleasure.

Perhaps the reader's patience is by this time exhausted, and I shall not detain him much longer; but I cannot dismiss the subject without making mention of some occurrences which have taken place since the first edition of my Narrative was published.

In the year 1798, my daughter Captive, and family, removed to the province of Lower Canada, which was no small grief to me. For the space of forty years, and upwards, we were together on the anniversary day of her birth, which was a great consolation to me, in my declining years.—And even after she was gone, although the distance was nearly two hundred miles, that anniversary day never passed unthought of or unnoticed by me, and I presume it never did by her, as she has often informed me since her return. The extraordinary occurrences of God's providence in preserving our lives through the various scenes which we passed in her infancy and childhood, might reasonably be supposed to attach that parental and dutiful affection to each other which could only be extinguished by the extinction of life.

My life, in many other respects, has been a scene of trouble and misfortune since I published my Narrative in 1796. Some time in October, in 1801, I had been on a visit to Mr. Samuel Taylor's in Rockingham; on my return, accompanied by his daughter, at the south end of the street in Charlestown our horse was started by a boy, wheeling a load of flax, which threw me from the horse. The violence of the fall was so great, together with a wound cut deep in my forehead, that I was taken up for dead, or apparently senseless, by my grand-son, Jason Wetherbee, and carried to the house of Samuel Stevens, Esq. about thirty rods. Every aid and assistance possible was made for me. After my revival, the wounds were dressed; the cut was sewed up by Mrs. Page, the wife of Capt. Peter Page of Charlestown. In a short time I so far recovered as to be removed to my home, which was nearly one mile. I recovered my former strength as soon as might be expected, considering the badness of the wound and bruises which I received by the fall.

My husband, Mr. John Hastings, with my consent and agreement, had prior to this time given our estate to Mr. Stephen Hasham, who married *our* only daughter. In consequence of which, my life and living were so immediately under his controul that my situation was rendered very unhappy. But a respect for the feeling of the surviving relatives will prevent my going into a detail of my sufferings, while under Mr. Hasham's roof; which, considering the different treatment I had a right to expect, under the care and protection of a son-in-law, I sometimes found almost as painful to be borne, as my savage captivity.

In the spring of 1803, my daughter Captive came from Canada, with a sick daughter of hers to be doctored, as physicians were at a great distance from where she resided. In the summer I made known to her my unhappy situation, as did my husband also. She, by the consent of my husband, and the advice of some respectable friends, procured a home for me at Mr. Jonathan Baker's, whose wife was daughter to my daughter Wetherbee, where I resided till February following; when, (with the assistance of Mr. Kimball and his brother who was in company with him on his journey to remove his wife and daughter to Canada) I was conveyed to Concord in Vermont, to Mr. Wetherbee's, my son-in-law, where I remained about ten months. We had intelligence in the early part of November that my husband was very sick; but the season and badness of the roads prevented my immediate return to see him. He died on the 21st day of November, 1804, in the —— year of his age.

In the January following I came to Charlestown, when, by the assistance of Mr. Wetherbee and others, I concluded a settlement with Mr. Hasham, in which I received the rents of certain pieces of land yearly, to continue during my natural life, which is sufficient to support me comfortably, and I can expend it where I please. I made my principal residence at Mrs. Rice's, who is a niece of mine, and sometimes with Mr. Wetherbee, my grandson, and visited my other relations, and was in as good health as might be expected for a person of my years.

I would here gladly close my narrative, but I have one more sad event to detail. In March, 1808, Mr. Kimball and family returned from Canada, and made their residence in Langdon, adjoining Charlestown; to which place I removed to reside with them, where I enjoyed myself happily with my daughter Captive, and her family, for about eighteen months; sometimes making visits among my many relatives and acquaintances, as it was convenient. In October, 1809, for to make it more convenient for Mr. Kimball to carry on his mechanical business, I concluded to make a short visit to Charlestown to spend the winter at my old quarters with Mrs. Rice. Accordingly on the 14th of October, set out for that purpose, in company with Mr. Kimball and Mr. John Sartwell, in whose waggon we all rode. We had not proceeded far from Mr. Sartwell's house, when, descending down a small pitch in the road, the staple drew out of the yoke, and let the spire drop, and the waggon pushing upon the horses, and striking their heels, soon set them out upon the run. The waggon, by some means or other, immediately upset, and came completely bottom up; so suddenly also, that it caught all three of us under it. In this situation we were dragged, as nearly as could be ascertained afterwards, by the blood, about six rods; when, by some cause or other, the waggon hoisted so as to let us out from under it. The horses soon cleared themselves from the waggon, and run about a half a mile. We were all, as must be expected, very much hurt. Mr. Sartwell had no bones broke, but was very much bruised, so that he was confined for some time. Mr. Kimball had one shoulder dislocated, and two fingers taken off from his left hand, besides being otherwise bruised. He can now use only his thumb and little finger of his left hand, the finger next to the little one being stiff. I had one ankle broken and the bone very much shattered, besides being otherwise bruised. I was carried back on a bier to my son Kimball's, where we both lay several weeks, and endured much excruciating pain. When I was laid on the bier to be carried back, it brought fresh to my mind the bier that the Indians made for me after the birth of my daughter Captive. It was thought by many, and I was even apprehensive myself, that the pain I endured, together with my age, would have proved too hard for me. But by the blessing of God, my life is still preserved, and I am once more restored to as comfortable a measure of health as I can expect with my years.* I am now in the winter of life, and feel sensibly the effects of old age. I have removed back to Charlestown, as also my daughter Captive, and her family. It is a matter of great consolation to me that I have it in my power to spend so much of my time with her in my latter days. I have had many a sorrowful hour on her account, in her infancy and childhood, and she has richly repaid them in her tender affection to me in my eve of life.

Instances of longevity are remarkable in my family. My aged mother, before her death, could say to me, arise daughter, and go to thy daughter; for thy daughter's daughter has got a daughter; a command which few mothers can make and be obeyed.

And now, kind Reader, after sincerely wishing that your days may be as happy as mine have been unfortunate, I bid you adieu.

Charlestown, September 10, 1810†.

---

*'Tis with satisfaction that I here express my unfeigned thanks to Doct. Kitteridge and Doct. Carpenter, for their particular attention to me during my confinement.—Also to the Rev. A. Kneeland for his prayers, and frequent visits during the same. It also gives me much satisfaction in reflecting (although my pains were almost intolerable) that my daughter Captive was able to attend me, which she did with her wonted cheerfulness, although many times I was fearful it might prove too hard for her health and constitution.

†NOTE.—Mrs. Johnson died in November, 1810, soon after the close of the foregoing Narrative.

APPENDIX.

THE Subject of the foregoing Narrative lived but a short time after the last date. She was very anxious to have this work revised and republished before her death. She had several conversations with me on the subject, while she lived in Langdon, and wished me to undertake the work, and get the copyright secured to her daughter Captive (Mrs. Kimball); which I told her I would do if time and opportunity would permit. But the sad accident and misfortune she met with soon after, as has been mentioned, together with other circumstances, prevented its being done at that time. I was in Charlestown, (Mass.) at the time of her death; and on my return home was informed by Col. Kimball, that it was the earnest desire of the old lady in her last sickness, that I should attend her funeral, and preach a sermon on the occasion; which sermon she wished to have annexed to her Narrative, as I had undertaken to revise the copy, and had not completed it. My being absent at the time of her death prevented the compliance with her request. But that I might in some measure comply with her wishes, and being particularly solicited by Col. Kimball, whose wife is the daughter

Captive, so often mentioned in the narrative, I preached a sermon on their account, at Langdon, on the 10th of February, 1811, and have annexed the substance of it to the narrative, by way of appendix.

A sermon is also added which was preached by the Rev. Dan Foster, late of Charlestown, at the funeral of Mrs. Whitcomb, formerly Mrs. Willard, the mother of Mrs. Johnson, *alias* Mrs. Hastings, the subject of this narrative.

I would further remark that this narrative has been considerably enlarged from papers furnished me by Col. Kimball, together with what I had previously taken from Mrs. Hastings' own mouth, and also the circumstance of the accident which happened at Langdon, which I was knowing to myself, and I believe the whole to be a correct statement of facts.

ABNER KNEELAND.

Langdon, Sept. 18, 1811.

A SERMON,

*Occasioned by the Death of Mrs. Hastings, who died Nov. 27th, 1810, in the eighty-first year of her age.**

TEXT—Eccl. xi. 8.

But if a man live many years, and rejoice in them all; yet let him remember the days of darkness, for they are many.

IT will be proper just to premise that the occasion of reading these words at this time is the late death of the aged and honorable Mrs. Hastings; a person with whom many of you, my hearers, have been long acquainted; and many more, if not all, have been made familiar with the narrative of her captivity and unparalleled sufferings; and your feeling sensibility has often been excited with the perusal, or recital, of those trying scenes through which she was called to pass, in the first settlement of this country.

To dilate, therefore, on her life or character, would be useless at this time (as it would be nothing new) to you who are present, and

---

*She breathed out her last expiring moments, till life was extinct, supported in the arms of her daughter Captive, for whom she ever manifested the greatest affection.

if this discourse should ever be more exten-
sively known, the most essential and important parts of her life will go with it. And as
she has bid the world adieu, and the most
solemn scene of her funeral is already past, it
will not so much be expected that I should
enter into those particulars at this time. Suf-
fice it therefore to say, that, having lived to a
good old age—having experienced many of
the various dispensations of the providence of
God—in prosperity, and in adversity—in joy,
and in sorrow—she has at last resigned her
worn out life, with a firm hope of a future immortality.

Happy indeed should I have been, to have
complied with her wishes so far as to have attended her interment, and delivered this discourse to her surrounding relations and friends
who attended on the solemn occasion. But
as my absence at the time prevented it, we
shall now dispense with any addresses that
might then have been thought proper, and
shall only attend to a doctrinal disquisition of
the text.

"But if a man live many years, and rejoice
in them all; yet let him remember the days
of darkness, for they are many."

The mortality of man is such, that but a
very few, comparatively speaking, live to what
is called *old age*. There are so many casual-
ties incident to human nature, that the pros-

pect of living "many years," is rendered doubtful and very uncertain. By an attention to the bills of mortality, it will be seen that the number who arrive to three score years and ten (what is called the common age of man) is but very small in comparison with the whole that are born; and although some by reason of strength live to four score years and upwards, yet is that strength labor and sorrow; for it is soon cut off and we fly away.

Virtue itself does not shield a man against the natural evils incident to human life. And though some may seem to have more of a full share than others, yet no one ought to expect wholly to avoid them.

We are not, however, to estimate a man's moral character by what outwardly befalls him; because time and chance must happen to all men; and if we wish to learn the real character of a man, we must notice with what patience, with what fortitude and resignation he endures the adverse scenes of life. And likewise his faithfulness in performing his duty, though in the midst of peril and danger.

Passing over the uncertainty of human life, which is apparent to all, I shall notice but two propositions from the text. And shew,

I.   What is necessary to enable a man to rejoice in all his days. And

II.   That the sorrows and afflictions incident to human nature are not incompatible with the joys of a christian.

I. What is necessary to enable a man to rejoice in all his days?

1. In order to pass through life comfortably and happy, and rejoice in all the dispensations of the providence of God, it is necessary that we should be made to know that "all things work *together* for *good*," though manifested only "to them that love God; to them that are called according to his purpose" —that the knowledge, the wisdom, the power, and even the love, or goodness of God, extends to all events, even to the most minute circumstances in his providential dealings with the children of men—that no event can take place without his divine permission, and that what he permits, all circumstances considered, is best so to be—that there is no calculating upon any thing in this lower world, as being certain to us, but *death*, and even *that* the time when is uncertain. That through the weakness of our understanding, the short sightedness of our knowledge, (every thing we see being temporal) although the order of things is unalterably fixed in the eternal mind, yet, to us, they are mutable, and therefore liable to change. And if we have been enabled to extend our thoughts so far as to discover the immutability of things in God, it is necessary that we should know that they

are immutably *good;* for how can a rational being rejoice in an unalterable evil? And furthermore, it increases our felicity to know that all things are not only established for good, but that they are established on rational principles; not by a blind chance, not simply by an unavoidable fate—for even good conferred upon us upon such principles, would not excite our gratitude to God, any more than a prize ticket drawn to us would excite our gratitude to the managers of the lottery: but the good which we receive is established by God himself, as being the fruits of infinite wisdom, effected by unlimited power, and prompted by unbounded love or goodness. And if we are rationally convinced that all events are wisely determined, it does not militate against our peace or happiness, to suppose, that the providence of God respecting them is immutably and unalterably established. For when any thing is once ordered for the *best*, it cannot be altered for the *better;* because there is nothing better than the best.

That the foreknowledge of God extends to all events, and that he overrules, superintends and governs all events, are truths that will not be disputed or denied by any who believe in a Supreme Being. And if we acknowledge that God governs all events, we must acknowledge that he governs them all for the best, or else we must acknowledge that he governs all

events, but not, or at least, not *all* of them for
the best; which idea would be blasphemously
absurd.

The Pharisees, when Christ was here in
the flesh, were reminded by him of their blas-
phemy; when, because they could not deny
the miracles which he wrought, they accused
him of having an unclean spirit, and that he
cast out devils through Beelzebub, the prince
of the devils. And the idea that God does, or
ever will punish his creatures, but not for their
good, is equally derogatory of his character.
Such ideas do not become the faithful child of
God. He rejoices that God overrules and
superintends all events, and that, however
grievous they may be to be borne, they are
wisely calculated to yield the peaceable fruits
of righteousness to them that are exercised
thereby.

This is the christian's consolation. Such
faith as this is able to solace the deepest affliction, and give patience and fortitude to the
mind. It strengthens the understanding and
gives vigilance to the animal faculties, so as
to enable us to go through any pain, peril or
danger, when prudentially deemed expedient,
to preserve our own lives or the lives of others.
A firm confidence in God is therefore absolutely necessary to enable us to rejoice, or
even calmly to acquiesce in the dispensations
of his providence.

2. A constant and inflexible adherence to the principles of virtue is also absolutely necessary to enable us to rejoice in all our days.

That a deviation from this principle should produce guilt, pain, condemnation, horror and remorse, appears to be one of the unalterable laws of moral nature. In vain may a man attempt to assuage his guilt, or calm his conscience with the idea that *he could not have done otherwise*, when he intends to do, or in fact has done, that which his own conscience tells him is wrong. For his guilt and all the evil consequences that follow, are as morally certain, as his crime. The carnal mind always reasons, if he attempts to reason at all, contrary to facts and our daily experience. He would willingly admit the moral certainty of all events if he could thereby exculpate himself from *blame*. And of course the carnal mind will argue thus; that he was under the fatal necessity of doing as he did: hence the blame, if any there be, cannot be in the creature. Not realizing that *guilt*, and all the evil consequences of sin, are as much *events*, in the providence of God, as the *crimes* that produce them. And it being consistent with infinite wisdom and goodness to suffer, permit or allow, sin to exist in the moral system, certainly it cannot be inconsistent with the same wisdom and goodness, even to *decree* that guilt and misery should be its direful consequences. For one, I am so fully convinced that virtue produces its own reward, and sin carries with it its own punishment, that I will venture to give it as a maxim, which I believe will ever hold true, that whatsoever produces no guilt, no shame, no remorse, no condemnation, in a word, no evil consequences, even to the sinner himself, is not sin. It may, however, be stated here, by way of objection, that a man may wrong his neighbor, or friend, without producing any injury to himself, and that such an act is sin. I grant that it is sin for any one man, knowingly, to injure another, or to give unjust or unnecessary pain, even to an enemy; but I deny the possibility of his doing it without producing the greatest injury to himself; and such a proposition ought to be first proved before it is taken for granted. One man may be the occasion of disturbing the peace of many; but he never can, by his own act, be the cause of the guilt of any but himself. It is true he may, by his evil example, induce others to commit the same crime, and thereby become equally guilty; but they are not guilty till they follow the evil example. And my hearers will be capable of judging which is the greatest misery, *sorrow* occasioned by the evil conduct of others, or *guilt* produced by our own crimes. My conscience tells me that the latter is the most to be dreaded.

My maxim is equally good on the side of
virtue. That which produces no peace, no
comfort, no consolation, in a word, no good
consequences, even to the *doer* of the deed, is
not virtue. And furthermore, whoever be-
stows a favor, on another, is the greatest par-
taker of the benefit; because "*it is more
blessed to give than to receive.*" If this senti-
ment be correct, as I presume it is, how blessed
indeed must be our heavenly Father, who is
the giver and bestower of every good and perfect gift, both spiritual and temporal. And
how miserable indeed must be the condition
of that man who is entirely destitute of a
principle of benevolence! Whoever, therefore,
would see good days, and rejoice in them all,
must adhere, rigidly adhere, to the strictest
observance of virtue. All outward professions,
without this internal principle, are but a mere
name, as empty in its sound as the "sounding
brass or the tinkling cymbal." He, and he
only, let him live many years or few, that keep-
eth a conscience void of offence towards God
and man, may be truly said to rejoice in all
his days.

3. Hope in immortality is also necessary to
enable a man to rejoice in all his days.

Short of this hope, the best prospects in life
are but an awful uncertainty. One thought
of death blasts all our expectations in this life,
as it respects ourselves, and a gloomy, dismal

and uncertain hereafter, is the only refuge to all those who have not a well grounded hope in immortality.

This hope is obtained only by a firm belief in the religion of Jesus Christ. In him, life and immortality are brought to light through the gospel. And whoever can fully believe (and whoever feels interested enough to examine the testimony will not doubt of the fact) that God raised up Jesus from the dead, can, from the same source of evidence, easily believe that the same power will raise up *us* also, and make us sit together with him, in heavenly places. "For if God spared not his own Son, but delivered him up for us all, how shall he not also with him freely give us all things?" —"who hath blessed us with all spiritual blessings, according as he hath chosen us in him, before the foundation of the world, that we should be holy and without blame before him in love." "Whoever hath this hope in him, (i. e. in Christ) will purify himself even as he is pure." And from the purity of his life and conduct he will be enabled to rejoice in all his days.

When we can, amidst all the trials, losses, crosses, affliction and disappointments incident to human life, look, by an eye of faith, beyond all death and time into that spiritual world, where sorrow can never come, and there, through the testimony of the mouth of

God's holy prophets, behold the "*ransomed of the Lord* returning and coming to him with songs and everlasting joys upon their heads, where they shall obtain joy and gladness, and sorrow and sighing shall flee away;" and through the fullness of the gospel, believe that Christ "gave himself a *ransom for all* to be testified in due time," will view all such afflictions but momentary; and therefore will receive them as specimens of the wisdom and goodness of our heavenly father, being calculated to work out for us "a far more exceeding and eternal weight of glory." Hence every bitter has its sweet, every sorrow is tempered with the spirit of consolation; and we have every reason to believe that as our day is, so will our strength be, and that while we are destined to live in this world, God will lay no more upon us than what he will enable us to bear. All pain must be either tolerable or intolerable—if tolerable, it may be endured—but if intolerable, it must be short—for the moment that pain becomes intolerable it destroys all sense, and therefore ceases to be pain.

Such faith, such hope, and such confidence in God will be sufficient to bear up the soul under all trials, carry it through all difficulties, giving it the final victory over sin and death.

4. As all mankind have sinned and come short of the glory of God, in order for us to get the victory over the sting of death, which

is sin, it is necessary that we should know that "God is in Christ reconciling the world unto himself, not imputing unto them their trespasses, but hath made him to be sin (or rather a sin offering) for us, who knew no sin, that we might be made the righteousness of God in him." And as repentance and remission of sins are necessary to reconciliation, God hath exalted Jesus to be "a Prince and a Savior, to give repentance unto Israel and remission of sins." And is he the God of the Jews only? Is he not the God of the Gentiles also? Yes of the Gentiles also. For God who is rich in mercy hath "concluded them all in unbelief that he might have mercy upon all." A remission, therefore, of all our sins that are past, and a salvation from sin for the future, is also necessary to enable us to rejoice in all our days. This brings me to shew,

Secondly. That the sorrows and afflictions incident to human nature, are not incompatible with the joys of a christian.

"Although affliction cometh not forth of the dust, neither doth trouble spring out of ground, yet man is born unto trouble, as the sparks fly upward." And although some are called to pass through much greater scenes of sorrow and affliction than others, yet there are none wholly exempt. In this respect, "time and chance happen unto all men."— "All things come alike to all: there is one event to the righteous and to the wicked; to the good, and to the clean, and to the unclean; to him that sacrificeth, and to him that sacrificeth not." Virtue, morality, religion, yea, even piety itself, does not exempt mankind from any natural evil to which we are subject. Neither is sin certain to produce any of those misfortunes to which we are always liable by the providence of God. If therefore there be no certain and necessary connexion between virtue and prosperity in the things of this world, and sin and adversity, or the misfortunes of life, then there is nothing that necessarily debars us from partaking of all the joys of a christian, notwithstanding our temporal life may be a scene of sorrow and affliction.

The original organization and constitution of the human body is sufficient to convince any rational mind, that is not fettered with the prejudices of a false education, that these bodies were never designed for an immortal state; for "flesh and blood cannot inherit the kingdom of God, neither can corruption inherit incorruption." Mortality is instamped upon all animated nature; and man, in this respect, hath no pre-eminence above a beast. "For that which befalleth the sons of men befalleth beasts; even one thing befalleth them: as the one dieth, so dieth the other; yea, they have all one breath."* Has sin affected the

*Eccl. iii. 19.

brutal creation, and produced their mortality ?
Or was man mortal and subject to death even
before sin entered the moral system? It is
true it was not revealed unto Adam that he
was dust, and must return to the dust again,
till after the transgression; but it was as true
before as it was afterwards; for the Lord God
formed man of the dust of the ground—gave
him an earthly constitution, which was sen-
sual, corruptible, yea, mortal. The evils of
mortality, therefore, ought not to be imputed
to sin. I am willing to grant that the miseries
of this mortal state may be greatly increased
by sin. But what I would wish to be under-
stood to say, is, that the seeds of mortality
were sown in man in the original constitution
of his nature, and that he was ever, after being
formed of the dust, subject to natural death;
and must have experienced the natural evils
attendant on this life, such as pains, sickness,
providential misfortunes, and even natural
death, if man had never sinned.

Again. It is said of Jesus, that "he shall
save his people from their sins." And if he
will save them from their sins, it is most
rational to believe that by so doing he will
save them all from the consequences of sin.
But Christ has never yet saved, and we have
no reason to expect that he ever will save, a
soul from natural death.

Christ himself, although without sin, was

subject to natural death. Death reigned from
Adam to Moses, even on those who had not
sinned after the similitude of Adam's transgression. And death still is and ever has been
the common lot of all animated nature, Enoch
and Elijah excepted. And I should consider
those two instances as early intimations of an
immortal state, rather than an evidence that
man originally was not subject to natural
death.

Much more might be said to establish this
proposition, if it were necessary; but our ar-
gument does not rest wholly on this particular
point; for even should we admit that natural,
as well as moral death is the effect of sin; yet
when we reflect that we have an advocate with
the Father, even Jesus Christ the righteous,
"who gave himself a propitiation for our sins,
and not for ours only but for the sins of the
whole world," we can anticipate the time when
all the consequences of sin, whether natural
or moral, will be completely at an end, and
death swallowed up of life.

Such a remembrance of the *days of darkness*
as this will serve to sweeten all our enjoyments
and give a zest to every real pleasure. We
should remember the evil days only to en-
hance our joys at the sight of deliverance, to
brighten our hopes in the prospect of future
glory, and to excite our gratitude for the un-
merited blessing. And such considerations

should further serve to give us fortitude of
mind to endure providential evils with patience and resignation while they continue.

The sentiments inculcated in this discourse
have been completely verified in the thor-
oughly tried life and unshaken death of her
who has been the occasion of it. She has gone
down to the dust in a good old age, like a
shock of corn fully ripe, richly laden with the
experience of the goodness of God. Her fortitude has been remarkable; and to this, under the providence of God, perhaps may be
imputed the preservation of her life through
scenes the most unparalleled of which history affords. Where one would have survived,
it is more than probable that hundreds would
have suffered death under more favorable
circumstances.

Her sufferings have been so great that many
who have read her Narrative have believed
the whole to be a fiction—a mere idle tale published to amuse the credulous part of commu-
nity, and get their money. But the additional
circumstances in the latter part of her life, together with her death, will give new strength
to the evidence and make her narrative still
more interesting. The plain simple facts
were sufficiently interesting, not to need the
imagination of the poet, or the eloquence of
the orator, to engage the attention of every
feeling heart.

The last respects to her remains have been
paid. She has paid the last debt of nature,
which we must all pay sooner or later. An
effecting stroke, to be sure, to her surviving
children and friends, though nothing more
than what they have long had reason to expect.
After surviving so many trying scenes, from
all of which she had recovered, she calmly
resigned her life, apparently being worn out
with old age. You have therefore, my respected friends, no serious cause to mourn;
but rather may you rejoice, that the earthly
house of her tabernacle being dissolved, you
have every reason to believe that she hath a
building of God, an house not made with
hands, eternal in the heavens.

She is gone to the world of spirits, and
thither must we all follow her sooner or later,
"For the dust must return to the earth as it
was, but the spirit to God who gave it." May
we all so live, and so conduct, whilst the brit-
tle thread of life is lengthened out unto us,
and also may we possess that faith, hope and
confidence in our God, that when he shall call
us to bid adieu to the things of time and
sense, we may go on our way rejoicing; be
enabled to look back on our past lives with
the pleasing satisfaction that we have kept a
conscience void of offence, toward God and
toward man; having our work done and well
done, which was allotted us here to do: may

we have nothing to do but to die—calmly falling asleep in Jesus Christ; may we close our eyes in peace on all sublunary enjoyments —rest in hope, till we shall arise to a glorious immortality—be clothed upon with our house from above, and be received into those realms of celestial glory, where no sin nor sorrow shall ever enter; there may our hearts be tuned upon the golden lyre of God's grace, to join with seraphs and angels and all the beatified spirits of the ransomed of the Lord which shall compose the heavenly hosts, to celebrate the praises of Him who is worthy to receive all possible glory, honor and power, throughout an ever beginning, and never ending eternity. Which may God grant to be the happy lot and portion of all the ransomed sons and daughters of Adam, for the sake of the " Mediation between God and men, the man Christ Jesus, who gave himself a *ransom* for all to be testified in due time, to whom with God the Father of our Lord Jesus Christ, "who hath blessed us with spiritual blessings," be ascribed all honor and glory, now, henceforth and forever more. Amen.

The Burial of a Mother.

BEHOLD the sad impending stroke!
  Which now arrests our eyes;
The silken bands of union broke,
  A tender Mother dies!

She's gone! She's gone to realms above!
  Where saints and angels meet;
To realize her Saviour's love,
  And worship at his feet.

Her pains and groans are now all o'er,
  She's gone to God on high;
Her wishful eyes shall weep no more,
  No more her spirit sigh.

For you who round her body mourn,
  And drop the flowing tears;
How many sorrows she hath borne,
  In all her lengthened years.

Her sorrows now are at an end,
  The Lord did for her call;
And Jesus is her only friend;
  Her life, her health, her ALL.

A SERMON,

Delivered at the funeral of Mrs. Whitcomb*,
May 7th, 1797;—By Dan Foster, A.M.

1 Cor. xv. 57.

"But thanks be to God who giveth us the victory through
our Lord Jesus Christ."

WERE it not for the hope of eternal life
given us in Christ Jesus, the departure of near
friends and relatives, and the thoughts of
death, would be accompanied with sorrows
almost insupportable. To be as though we
never had been, at best is but a gloomy
thought: but an eternal existence in sin and
misery is a thought infinitely more intolerable.
Any thing short, then, of possessing the hope
of life and immortality, promised in the gospel,
would render all beyond the grave, at best,
but a sad and awful uncertainty. And altho'
the christian has no positive demonstration,
as it is necessary, whilst he tabernacles in the
flesh, that he should walk "by faith and not
by sigh⁺," yet, relying on the divine testimony,
he possesses a hope that is like an "anchor
to his soul," both sure and stedfast; which
hope entereth into that which is within the
vail, where Jesus, our propitiation and fore
runner, hath entered for us. This hope

---

*See page 138.

giveth us the victory, and enables us to triumph over the fear of death. I shall proceed, on this occasion, in the following order:

I.   I will endeavor to state the connexion of the words with the context, and shew the general instruction contained in the chapter.

II.   Make a practical use of the meaning of the text.

In the beginning of the chapter the apostle refers to the gospel which he had preached, and speaks of its nature and importance, as in verse 1—4. "Moreover, brethren, I declare unto you the gospel which I preached unto you, which also ye have received, and wherein ye stand; by which also ye are saved, if ye keep in memory what I preached unto you, unless ye have believed in vain. For I delivered unto you first of all, that which I also received, how that Christ died for our sins, according to the scriptures: And that he was buried, and that he rose again the third day, according to the scriptures." Hence it is evident the doctrine of the resurrection of the dead was contained in the gospel of Jesus Christ, which Paul preached. Yea, the knowledge of salvation, the knowledge of God, whom to know is life eternal, comes to man through the medium of the gospel, which is "good tidings of great joy to all people."

Some of the most important articles of the gospel, which is our salvation, are these; that

"Christ died for our sins;" i. e. to procure the remission of them, to propitiate them, and reconcile us to God, "according to the scriptures." As the apostle observes, "if any man sin, we have an advocate with the Father, Jesus Christ the righteous: And he is the propitiation for our sins; and not for ours only, but also for the sins of the whole world." "For the love of Christ constraineth us because we thus judge; that if one died for all, then were all dead; and he died for all, that they who live should not live unto themselves, but unto him that died for them and rose again." Isaiah gives us the same idea of the design of the death of Christ: see chap. liii. ver. 5, 6. "But he was wounded for our transgressions; he was bruised for our iniquities; the chastisement of our peace was upon him; and with his stripes we are healed. All we, like sheep, have gone astray; we have turned every one to his own way; and the Lord hath laid on him the iniquity of us all."

We are not only taught, by the scriptures, that Christ died for our sins, but that he rose again, for our justification as the apostle elsewhere observes: "Who was delivered for our offences and rose again for our justification; therefore, being justified by faith, we have peace with God, through our Lord Jesus Christ: by whom also we have access by faith in this grace wherein we stand, and rejoice

in hope of the glory of God." In consequence
of the resurrection of Christ, the apostle, and
we, and all believers, are *justified* in having
faith in him as a divine person, the Messias,
of whom Moses and the prophets did write;
the Shiloh, who was to come; the Just One, to
whom the gathering of the people shall be;
the Lamb of God, who taketh away the sin of
the world; the Christ, who by the blood of
his cross shall reconcile all things unto himself; the Saviour, who shall save his people
from their sins; the Mediator, who gave himself a ransom for all to be testified in due time.
The apostle speaks of the resurrection of
Christ, as a matter of vast importance; and
as a thing of sufficient certainty. See the
importance attached to the resurrection of
Christ by the apostle, as expressed in the 17th
verse of the context. "And if Christ be not
raised, your faith is vain; ye are yet in your
sins."

If Christ arose not from the dead, we have
no reason to confide in him as a divine person, the Messias, the Mediator with God, the
Captain of our salvation; and we have no reason to expect reconciliation to God through
him; yea, we can have no hope in the resurrection of the dead; for the apostle expressly
says, "if the dead rise not, then is not Christ
raised." And according to the apostle's mode
of reasoning, (who was a good reasoner) if

Christ be not raised, then will the dead rise not, agreeably to the 18th verse—"Then they also which are fallen asleep in Christ are perished." But the apostle turns his hypothetical mode of reasoning into affirmative and positive assertions; as in verse 20th, and on;— "But now is Christ risen from the dead, and become the first fruits of them that slept. For since by man came death, by man came also the resurrection of the dead. For as in Adam all die, even so in Christ shall all be made alive. But every man in his own order: Christ the first fruits: afterward they that are Christ's at his coming. Then cometh the end, when he shall have delivered up the kingdom to God, even the Father; when he shall have put down all rule and all authority, and power. For he must reign, till he hath put all enemies under his feet. The last enemy that shall be destroyed is death." Thus we may see the importance attached to the death of Christ.

And the certainty of his triumphing over death, and reascending his native heaven, cannot be reasonably doubted, when we consider that he was actually seen alive, after his crucifiction, by many creditable witnesses. He was seen of Cephas, of the twelve, and afterwards of above five hundred at once; some of whom were fallen asleep, but many remained when Paul wrote the above testimony. And last of all he was seen of the apostle, who, in all his writings, and in the whole history of his life, appears to have been a man of good abilities, considerable literature, and of a sound, strong mind, not addicted to enthusiastic flights, but in all his reasoning appealed to incontestible facts, as the foundation of his arguments, which he knew were incontrovertible, and must be acknowledged by his opponents.

Another important article of the gospel of our salvation, is, that human bodies shall rise again. "This corruptible shall put on incorruption, and this mortal shall put on immortality." "For we are not appointed unto wrath, but to obtain salvation." So we see that man is appointed to obtain salvation through Jesus Christ. See verse 19th of the context—"If in this life only we have hope in Christ, we are of all men the most miserable." See also the 20th verse, and on, before quoted. How glorious a discovery this! What a display of gospel grace! This mortal shall put on immortality! That which is sown in weakness shall be raised in power; that which is sown a natural body shall be raised a spiritual body; that which is sown in dishonor shall be raised in glory!

Another most important article of the gospel which St. Paul preached, is this, that Jesus, the Son of God, the Saviour of the world, shall sway the mediatorial sceptre, till all the enemies of the moral administration of Jehovah shall be subdued, and brought into voluntary, cheerful subjection. "For he," that is Christ, "must reign, till he hath put all enemies under his feet. The last enemy that shall be destroyed is death. For he," that is God Supreme, God the Father of all, "hath put all things under his," that is, under Christ, the Son's, "feet." But when he saith, All things are put under him, it is manifest that he, the Father, "is excepted, which did put all things under him," the Son. "And when all things shall be subdued unto him," the Son, "then shall the Son also himself be subject," made like unto his brethren, "unto HIM that put all things under *him*, that God may be all in all."

The apostle then proceeds to state, what has been before noticed, the surprising transformation of human bodies at the resurrection. See verses 42, 44.—"So also is the resurrection of the dead; it is sown in corruption, it is raised in incorruption; it is sown in dishonor, it is raised in glory; it is sown in weakness, it is raised in power; it is sown a natural body, it is raised a spiritual body."

O how great, how glorious will this change be, of our poor, frail, mortal bodies!

The apostle next proceeds to speak of the change which living men shall experience,

when Christ shall come again, and the celestial
trumpet shall raise the dead. See verse 51—
53.—"Behold, I shew you a mystery; We
shall not all sleep, but shall all be changed, in
a moment, in the twinkling of an eye, at the
last trumpet, for the trumpet shall sound, and
the dead shall be raised incorruptible, and *we*
shall be changed. For this corruptible *must*
put on incorruption, and this mortal must put
on immortality." This will be a great, and
an instantaneous change of corruptible for incorruption, and of mortal for immortality, of
which we can now have no adequate conception. When this great and mighty change
shall take place, then shall be the destruction
of temporal or bodily clay: see verse 54.—
"So when this corruption shall have put on
incorruption, then shall be brought to pass the
saying that is written, Death is swallowed up
in victory." The glorious truths that will
also be brought to pass in connexion with this
saying, "Death is swallowed up in victory,"
we have recorded in the prophecy of Isaiah,
chap. xxv. ver. 6—8. "And in this mountain shall the Lord of hosts make unto all people a feast of fat things, a feast of wines on
the lees; of fat things full of marrow, of wines
on the lees well refined. And he will destroy
in this mountain the face of the covering cast
over all people, and the vail that is spread over
all nations. He will swallow up death in

victory; and the Lord God will wipe away tears from off all faces; and the rebuke of his people shall he take away from off all the earth: for the Lord hath spoken it." So we see that this glorious feast that shall be made unto *all people*, is to be fulfilled, according to the sense of the apostle, when this mortal shall have put on immortality, and this corruptible is clothed with incorruption. In confirmation of this glorious truth, the Revelator hath said, Rev. xxi. 3, 4—"Behold, the tabernacle of God is (or shall be) with men, and he will dwell with them, and they shall be his people, and God himself shall be with them, and be their God. And God shall wipe away all tears from their eyes; and there shall be no more *death*, neither sorrow nor crying, neither shall there be any more pain: for the former things are passed away."

The apostle then tells us what creates the terrors of a dying scene, even sin against the laws of God. See verse 56.—"The sting of death is sin; and the strength of sin is the law." Then follow the words of the text.—"But thanks be to God which giveth us the victory through our Lord Jesus Christ."

II. As a practical improvement of the text, we may consider, 1. What death is, with some of its accidents and consequences: 2. How Christ hath mitigated its terrors, and given us the victory over it; and take notice of

our obligations to him for so inestimable
a favor.

1. Death, as it respects only our body, is
the extinction of our mere animal life; which
is common to man, beasts, birds, creeping
things, and all animated nature; and is generally attended with great and exquisite pain
and distress. This is evident (except when the
cause is too sudden to be felt) from apparent
circumstances; and also as it is reasonable to
suppose, upon so great an effect as will cause all
the vital powers, and every coarser and finer
nerve of the human frame, to cease to operate.

Our bodies, at death, are left with our
friends to be interred in the cold and silent
earth, and to crumble and moulder back to
their primordinal dust. "Then shall the dust
return to the earth as it was; and the spirit
shall return unto God who gave it."

At death we close our eyes on all this transi-
tory world, and the changing scenes of things.
We bid adieu, for a longer or a shorter time,
as God shall please, to kindred, friends and
neighbors—to all the joys, all the sorrows,
and all the trifles of time and sense.

Death transmits our souls into the presence,
of our Maker, and into a new and unexperi-
enced scene of things of which we can now
form but very imperfect ideas.

But as we are moral and accountable beings,
so it is the scriptural idea that death is suc-

ceeded by our actual appearance in the more
immediate and sensible presence of God and
the Lamb, of whom we shall receive such sen-
tence and appointment as will be consistent for
a Being of infinite goodness, justice, mercy,
love and truth, to give.

Of the process of this personal interview
and examination before God and the Lamb,
which taketh away the sin of the world, we
are greatly unacquainted; though, as a certain consequence of death, we have the utmost
reason to expect it. Here, "we know in part,
and we prophesy in part, but when that which
is perfect is come, then that which is in part
shall be done away." "Therefore, judge
nothing before the time, until the Lord come,
who both will bring to light the hidden things
of darkness, and will make manifest the coun-
sels of the heart; and then shall every man
have praise of God."—1 Cor. xiii. 9, 10.—
iv. 5.

After this important interview with our
Maker, we shall enter into that society, and
upon the employments and enjoyments—or
into that state of suffering and punishment
inseparably connected with sin*—to which we

---

*The reader will here notice that Mr. Foster held to
the doctrine of future punishment, though he believed
in the final restoration of all rational intelligences to ho-
liness and happiness. These are his words:—"I frank-
ly declare to you, that I feel myself disposed to extend

shall be destined by infinite wisdom and goodness.

2. How Christ hath mitigated the terrors of death, and given us the victory over it; with our obligations to him for so inestimable a favor.

After the apostle had plainly told us what created the terrors of death, even sin, and what gave sin its terrific efficacy, even the law of God, he devoutly thanks God that he hath given christians the victory over death, i. e. had removed its terrors, and unclothed it of its dreadful appearance and frightful garb, &c. through Jesus Christ.

Hence, by the help of our context, we may discover what Christ hath done to free us from the dread and terror of a dying hour.

1. "He hath died for our sins."

Though we are sinners, we are sure of pardon, peace and reconciliation with God, thro' the merits of the Saviour! For Christ came

---

the divinely benevolent design of gospel grace and mercy, in such a manner, as to include all the children of Adam. Nor can I possibly understand any definitions of the divine attributes, or interpretations of the declarations of the gospel itself, upon any other supposition of the extent of gospel grace and mercy. For this theory of the divine attributes and moral government, and extent of gospel grace and mercy, I am willing to write, to preach, and to converse, so long as I live, and shall be able to use my pen and tongue." See Foster's Examination page 289.

not to continue us *in* our sins, but to save us *from* our sins. "For he shall save his people from their sins." Reason dictates that this reflection must greatly mitigate the terror of death, and administer unspeakable comfort and consolation to the dying christian.

2. We have hope through Christ of a resurrection and a future life.

"If in this life only we have hope in Christ, we are of all men the most miserable." But glory to God for his rich and sovereign grace, we are not left to temporary hopes from Christ. "For as in Adam all die, even so in Christ shall all be made alive." The effects of divine grace shall be as extensive as those of Adam's sin. "For where sin hath abounded, grace doth much more abound."

When the dying christian reflects, that what he now sows in corruption, shall be raised in incorruption—what he sows in dishonor shall be raised in glory—what he sows in weakness shall be raised in power—what he sows a natural body shall be raised a spiritual body— with what divine consolation and glorious hope may he lay his body down to sleep in the dust, till God shall call it to celestial life!

Immortality, which was but conjectural by the wisest Pagan philosophers, is clearly preached by the gospel, and demonstrated by the resurrection of Christ.

What returns of grateful praise and sincere

obedience are due to God, who hath given us
the victory over death, by the clear and certain hope of a blessed immortality through
Jesus Christ.

3. All needful and divine assistance and
support, in a dying hour, may the christian
hope for through Jesus Christ.

Our flesh is so weak, our natural faculties
so frail and feeble, that after all the glorious
hopes of peace and pardon through the blood
of the everlasting covenant, and of a resurrection to life and immortality, when death shall
approach, we shall need the rod and staff of
God for our support. This also we may hope
for, since God hath assured us that he will
never leave us, nor forsake us.

IMPROVEMENT, by usual Addresses.

1. To the children, and other surviving
relatives of the deceased;

You, my respected friends, are now called
to attend the interment of the last remains
of a kind and tender parent, whose presence, comfort and assistance you have long
enjoyed.

This is, on many accounts, an affecting,
solemn scene. She was an head of one of
the earliest families who first settled this
town. Though she never was captivated,
nor received any personal injury from the

savages, yet she endured many hardships, and severe sufferings, on account of the injuries done to her connexions and friends, by the natives. A kind and indulgent husband, father of the children present, was presented to her a ghastly corpse, a victim of savage barbarity!—Oh the heart aching pangs your mother then endured! She also suffered on account of the captivity of three of her children;—of two of them for the long and painful term of three years, and a few months. But through the goodness of God, they were all returned to her joyful and grateful embraces again; and two of them are now alive and attending on this solemn occasion.

She was born April 24th, 1710, and died May 5th, 1797, having just entered her 88th year.

A numerous posterity hath descended from her; and, by her blood, or affinity, she was connected with a great part of the families in this town.

She left, at her death, two hundred and twenty-seven lineal descendants.

And permit me to add, that as your dear departed mother was an early settler in this town, she must have gone through a variety of troublesome scenes—experienced much of the goodness of God, and many adverse providences. She hath been a kind indulgent parent—an obliging neighbor—a faithful friend—specially kind and useful in times of sickness and distress, particularly in the infant days of this settlement.

I am averse to the general practice of giving characters in funeral avocations; or of being very positive of the *immediate* happy state of departed friends. But we have reason to hope that the goodness and mercy of God, in Christ Jesus, will admit to eternal rest and peace, a friend who hath seen and enjoyed, done and suffered so much, as your departed mother hath.

You will do well to attend to her good advices, and follow her good examples. Love God, and Christ, and religion. Remember that nothing but real religion can give you substantial comfort, when you come to die.

Remember that Christ hath conquered death, and disarmed him of his terrors: so that all those who believe in, and obey him, have nothing to fear from that source.

Look now, my respected friends, into the grave; it is the house appointed for you; for us all. Improve this providence to the glory of God; and let it awaken your attention to the things of eternal peace.

Be patient, submissive, resigned to God; and learn obedience by the things you suffer. May God be present with, assist and bless you, my dear friends; and sanctify this providence to you for your eternal good.

2. A few words to the whole congregation will close the subject.

You, my respected audience, are called to attend to the funeral solemnities of an aged neighbor, acquaintance and friend: one of the first inhabitants of this town; who saw it in its infancy, in its maturer years, and in its present state.

Many of you, my aged fathers and mothers, are far advanced in life, and must quickly follow this aged mother in Israel, whose remains we this day inter. Many reflections will, no doubt, enter your minds on this occasion; but none can be more solemn, or more important, than this, that you must quickly die. Reflect that it is God's design, in this providence, to admonish, and do you good. It is a call to you; —"Be ye also ready."

Remember, my fellow travellers, bound with me to a vast eternity, and improve the gladsome idea, that God hath given us the victory over death, through our Lord Jesus Christ; to whom be glory for ever. Amen.

Names of persons Killed in Charlestown, No. 4, and time when—by the Indians.

Seth Putnam, May 2, 1748.—Samuel Farnsworth, Joseph Allen, Peter Perin, Aaron Lyon, Joseph Massey, May 24, 1746.—Jedediah Winchel, June or July, 1746. —— Phips, August 3, 1746.—Isaac Goodale, Nathaniel Gould, October, 1747.—Obadiah Sartwell, June, 1749.—Lieut. Moses Willard, June 18, 1756.—Asahel Shebbins, August, 1758.—Josiah Kellogg, 1759.

Number taken Prisoners by the Indians, from Charlestown, No. 4.

Capt. John Spafford, Isaac Parker, Stephen Farnsworth, April 19, 1746. —— Anderson, October, 1747.—Enos Stevens, June 17, 1749.—James Johnson, Susanna Johnson, Sylvanus Johnson, Susan Johnson, Polly Johnson, Miriam Willard, Peter Labarree, Eben Farnsworth, August 29, 1754.—Sampson Colefax, David Farnsworth, Thomas Robins, Asa Spafford, May, 1756.—Mrs. Robins, Isaac Parker, David Hill, August, 1758. —Joseph Willard, wife and five children, June 7, 1760.

Letter from Col. Lydius to Mrs. Johnson.

Albany, May 5, 1755.
Mrs. Johnson—I received yours of the 6th

April, with one for your husband; it seems you are concerned whether or no he got safe here: it seems also by yours, that you mention to have received a letter from me, and none from your husband. When he left Albany to go to New-England, he left me a letter for you, to be forwarded the first opportunity, which I did with that you received from me. I have expected your husband this three months past, to come and fetch you and your family. Since he left Albany I never received a line from him, and the occasion of the delay I cannot conceive, without it is the difficulty to procure silver money. Keep good heart, I hope you will soon see your husband, is the wish from your humble servant,

JOHN W. LYDIUS.

———

From Col. Cuyler to Mr. James Johnson.

Albany, June 17, 1755.

SIR—I have received yours of the 7th and 8th inst. and have noted the contents. I really do not understand what you write me for in the first place—you say that my bills were not accepted—at the same time I find by your draught on me that you have received on my account 2300 livres, from Mr. La Corne St. Luc. I now send to him 438 dollars for the payment of your draught. I am sorry that Mr. Rine de Cauogne has not accepted of my bills, for several reasons. I have now desired La Corne St. Luc to let you have 700 livres besides the 2300 which you have already received. I am, sir, your humble servant.

CORNELIUS CUYLER.

————

From Mr. Johnson to Miss Miriam Willard.

Quebec, April 16, 1756.
Loving Sister—After our love to you, these are to inform you that we are all well at present, as I hope these will find you and our little daughter, and all other friends at Montreal. I have written to you once before now, and we have had no answer, so that we do not know what your circumstances are, only that the General was so good as to let us know that you and Susanna were well. I would have you go to the General and beg the favor to come down here to live with us; for I have written to the General, and begged the same favor. I would have you spare no pains, for if you meet with any misfortunes it will contribute very much to your parents' sorrow, as well as to ours. So I would not have you discouraged, or harbor any thoughts of staying in this country, for I do not doubt but we shall go home this summer; for I have

desired the General to send home those of us that are paid for, and will stay in the country till there is a change of prisoners: and if you cannot come down, beg leave of the General to let you write to us—let us know what your circumstances are. Give my services to Mr. Du Quesne and Madam, and to Susanna's mothers.—We remain your loving brother and sister.

JAMES & SUSANNA JOHNSON.

———

From Miss Miriam Willard to Mr.
Johnson.
(*Written at Montreal, July or August,* 1756)

Loving Brother and Sister,

Having received yours of the 5th July, it being the second, though you have sent four —wherein you give me to understand that my sister is not well, and that you would have me come down—for which I have asked the liberty of the General; he does not see fit to let me come, unless I would go to prison, and I think I am better off here than that comes to; therefore I take this opportunity to inform you of my health at this time, and of Susanna, and all the rest of the prisoners here, (and my love is folded up in their lives) with our friends that we were taken with, to you and to all friends there. Susanna has had the small pox, and is prodigiously marked.

I would not have you be concerned about my staying here, for the longer I stay the more anxious desires I have to go home.

MIRIAM WILLARD.

P. S.—I hear by Mr. Josiah Foster of Winchester, who was taken on the 7th of June, with his family, that our friends at No. 4 were all well, and our brother James was returning from the eastward.—No more at present—I shall subscribe myself in haste your loving sister,   M. W.

———

From Mr. Josiah Foster to Mr. Johnson.

Montreal, May 16, 1757.

SIR—After my respects to you, your wife, and sister, hoping you are in health, as we are at present, blessed be God for it. The 5th day of this present month, the Mohawks brought in prisoners from No. 4, Mr. David Farnsworth, Sampson Colefax, Deacon Adams, Asa Spafford, and George Robins, which gives us the sorrowful news of the death of your father Willard, who was killed by the Indians last summer a little way from the fort. Your brother Moses was stabbed in the thigh with a spear—this is all the mischief that has been done, except the Indians burnt the mills. Mr. Labarree has made his escape from Montreal, and has gone for the English fort. I should be glad to write you

a fuller account of things, but it is very diffi-
cult to write. I should be glad you would
write to me, to let me know how you are. So
I remain your friend,

JOSIAH FOSTER.

———

*From Mrs. Bisson to Mrs. Johnson, after her
return.*

Quebec, Sept. 15, 1757.
Madam—It is with all possible pleasure I
do myself the pleasure to write, and to let you
know the dullness I feel since your departure. One would not imagine it, considering
the little time I had the happiness to be acquainted with you. I wish I had it in my
power to convince you of the truth of it, but
the distance hinders us; you will know from
your husband how I have done all I could to
see he had done for him all the little services
in my power. I pray you would salute Miss
Miriam in my name, and tell her I wish her
a pretty little husband at her return, worthy
her merit. Embrace also your two little
misses; my daughter Mary Ann assures you
of her respects, and salutes kindly Miss Miriam and the two little Misses.—I beg you to
enquire after my son, who I believe is taken,
because he is so long before he comes home:
his name is James Bisson, son of James Bisson and Hubelle Badeau. I pray you again,

that in case you find him, to do him what service you can, and to take care of him: I shall be everlastingly obliged to you for it. I conclude by assuring you that I shall all my life be, Madam, one of your greatest friends, and your humble servant.

THE WIDOW BISSON.

Our neighbor, Miss Mary Ann Deforme assures you of her respects, and salutes Miss Miriam and the two little Misses. Miss Sinette and Tenesa Voyer assure you of their respects, and also Miss Mary Ann and the two Misses. Adieu, Madam Johnson—I wish you health and much joy upon Mr. Johnson's return, who is to depart from hence immediately.

———

PASSPORT—*By Gen. Monchton.*

Halifax, Oct. 19, 1757.

The bearer, Mr. James Johnson is at liberty to take his passage on Board any vessel bound to the continent.

ROBERT MONCHTON.

From Mr. Johnson to Mrs. Johnson.

Fort Edward, June 22, 1758.

My Dear—This day I have had the sorrowful news of the loss of my dear child.— May God sanctify this and all other of his

afflictive dispensations to us. I am in good
health at present, blessed be God for it, hoping this will find you and the rest of my dear
children in like manner. We are to march
tomorrow to the Lake. I have nothing remarkable to tell you—I am in haste, so I remain your most loving husband,

JAMES JOHNSON.

———

Charlestown, Jan. 10, 1799.
We, whose names are subscribed, having
been many years acquainted with Mrs. Hast-
tings, formerly Mrs. Johnson, who was captivated by the Indians in this town in the year
1754, are willing to say in her favor, that we
have ever considered her as a woman of verac-
ity, and that she hath ever sustained a good
character. Some of us were in town when
she was captivated, and none of us have reason to disbelieve the statement of facts which
she has given the public.

PETER LABARREE,
THOMAS PUTNAM,
MOSES WILLARD,
WILLIAM HEYWOOD,
JOSEPH WILLARD,
SYLVANUS HASTINGS,
TIMOTHY PUTNAM,
ABEL WALKER,
SAMUEL WETHERBE,
} Present when Mrs. Hastings was captivated.

SAMUEL TAYLOR,
TIMOTHY CARLETON,
OLIVER HASTINGS,
JONATHAN BAKER,
ELIJAH GROUT,
DEMELL GROUT,
BEZALEEL SHAW,
SETH GROUT,
WILLIAM GILBERT.

Captain Johnson's Commission.

Province of the Massachusetts Bay:
THOMAS POWNALL, Esq. Captain
General and Governor in Chief, in
and over his Majesty's Province of
L. S.   the Massachusetts Bay in New-
England, and Vice Admiral of the
same, &c.

To James Johnson, Esq.—*Greeting*
By Virtue of the Power and Authority in
and by His Majesty's Royal Commission to
me granted to be Captain General, &c. over
this His Majesty's Province of the Massachusetts Bay aforesaid, I do by these Presents
(reposing especial Trust and Confidence in
your Loyalty, Courage and Good Conduct)
Constitute and Appoint You the said James
Johnson to be Captain of a Company in the
Battalion of Light Infantry to be formed out

of the Forces now raised by me for a general Invasion of Canada, commanded by Colonel Oliver Partridge.

You are therefore carefully and diligently to discharge the Duty of a Captain in leading, ordering and exercising said Company in Arms, both inferior Officers and Soldiers, and to keep them in good Order and Discipline, and they are hereby commanded to obey you as their Captain; and you are yourself to observe and follow such Orders and Instructions, as you shall from time to time receive from the General and Commander in Chief of His Majesty's Forces in North America, your Colonel or any other your superior Officer according to the Rules and Discipline of War in pursuance of the Trust hereby reposed in You.

Given under my Hand and Seal of Arms at Boston, the thirtieth Day of March, in the thirty-first Year of the Reign of His Majesty King George the Second, Anno Domini, 1758.

T. POWNALL.

By His Excellency's Command,

A. OLIVER, *Secretary*.

FINIS

SCOUT JOURNALS.

1757.

NARRATIVE OF JAMES JOHNSON,
A Captive during the French and Indian Wars.

Edited and Annotated by
G. WALDO BROWNE.

1902.
MANCHESTER, N. H.

PRIVATELY PRINTED.

EDITION LIMITED TO ONE HUNDRED COPIES.

No. 19

Narrative of James Johnson.

A CAPTIVE DURING THE INDIAN WARS IN NEW ENGLAND.

COMPILED FROM THE MASSACHUSETTS ARCHIVES, VOL. 38 A, PAGE 329, AND ANNOTATED BY G. WALDO BROWNE.

SKETCH OF CAPTAIN JOHNSON.

Captain James Johnson was among the earlier settlers of Grant No. 4, now Charlestown, N. H., and came here from Massachusetts with others to help defend a post that was so favorably situated to guard one of the most common routes of the Indians on their way to and from Canada. The fort here was built by Massachusetts and was supposed to be in that province. On the morning of August 29, 1754, he and his family, consisting of his wife, three children and sister-in-law, Miriam Willard, were surprised by the Indians, and with two men named Peter Larabee and Ebenezer Farnsworth, were carried off captives. The long journey proved extremely trying, the party at times suffering for food. On the second day Mrs. Johnson gave birth to a child, a daughter christened Captive, from the conditions surrounding her birth. The captors appear to have been very solicitous of the welfare of their captives, and upon reaching Montreal, Johnson was given a parole of two months to enable him to return and solicit aid to redeem himself and the others. Appealing to the assembly of New Hampsire, he obtained, after a vexatious delay, one hundred and fifty pounds sterling. But the season had been well advanced before he had returned, and it was then winter, and he was unable to get back to Montreal before another spring. This gave his captors grounds to claim that he had broken his parole, and after being robbed of considerable of his money he was seized and thrown into prison, together with his wife, four children, and her sister. Remaining a year and a half in prison, Mrs. Johnson, two of her daughters, and her sister were sent to England, from whence they eventually reached Boston.   Captain Johnson was kept in prison three years, when he was allowed to go to Boston, accompanied by his son.   The other child, his eldest daughter, had been innured in a nunnery just out of Montreal, and he was unable to effect her release.   He and his son fortunately reached Boston in season to meet the fugitives from England, and after having passed through a series of hardships, sufferings and misfortunes peculiar to pioneer life, the distressed family were reunited, with the exception of the daughter mentioned, who never rejoined her kindred.   Still Captain Johnson's misfortunes were not entirely over, for he was soon arrested and thrown into prison charged with being in the employ of the French.   Happily he soon disproved this charge, and there is nothing to show that he experienced any further harm.

This account of personal adventures is valuable mainly for the information it contains regarding the distances, physical features of the country, and the association of the French and Indians.

DEPOSITION OF CAPTAIN JOHNSON [1]

The Committee who was directed to examine James Johnson, a Late Captain in Canada, beg leave to Report that he gives ye following account of facts (viz.) that it is a hundred miles from No. 4 to Crown Point that in his Journey to Canada [2] he

---

1. November 14, 1757.

2. This was the most common route of the Indians in their passages to the valley of the Connecticut below what was known as "Moose Meadows," now included in Haverhill and Piermont.   These highways of travel for the Indians always followed the most convenient waterways, and after following a stream to its fountain-head, if their course led as far, they loaded their burdens on their backs, including their canoes, and so crossed the country to the nearest river or pond lying in their course, In 1759, New Hampshire cut a road from the junction of Black River with the Connecticut at No. 4, across what is now the State of Vermont to the headwaters of Lake Champlain in order to open an easier route to Canada. This followed very closely the old Indian trail from Pocumtuck valley to Montreal.

Another trail of the red men was up the Connecticut River to Weld's, now Wells River, thence up that stream to its source in the Green Mountains, and through a gap in the highlands to the headwaters of the French now Lamoile River, after which a comparatively easy way was found to their destination.   A third route, more broken than either of the others, was taken usually by the Indians visiting the Merrimack valley as far south as Dunstable.   This followed the Merrimack and Pemegiwassett and Baker's Rivers to the dividing ridge between the valleys.   Thence by a "carrying-place," and small stream to the Connecticut, up that river to where is now the town of Dalton, thence striking across the western and northern country by small streams and lakes to the head of Lake Memphremagog, and down that body of water and outlet to the St. Francis River. Did they wish to keep on to Quebec the course was then down the St. Lawrence.

passed a River Called black River ye first night that he Crossed White River Several times and for want of a canoe he travel'd by otter Creek that in General the travelling was good that he could not tell how high the Emminence of Crown Point was but that the Citadle is the opposite side & before (.) ye breastwork was Raised Shot would strike ye Door of ye Citadel from ye Emminence & the wall of the fort is twelve feet high & twelve feet thick & then abreast work about Two foot thickness — (the) heights & ye Cannon are planted nearly alike Round the fort Excepting on part of ye north Square where ye barracks are (&) that there is no out works (&) that he apprehends the Citadel is not tenable against proper battering pieces and that the place of unloading their vessell from the fort is about Sixty Rod & the Emminence is a hundred Rod from ye place of unloading & before ye vessell Can be Covered by ye fort She must be Exposed to a fire from ye Emminence & that ye powder house Stores exposed to ye Emminence that there is no no well in ye fort that ye Store house is next to the Emminence that there is but one outer Gate & that has a Drawbridge before it & a Gate within that, which may be drawn up (&) drop'd down as occasion Requires that there is no (?)[3] in ye fort & but one vessel in ye lake[4] which is about 70 tons without guns & that from Crown Point he went to St Johns Fort at the other end of ye Lake and from there to Champlain River[5] & that from St Johns Fort to St Francis is about fifty miles near north & from St Francis to St Lawrence[6] is about five miles & that ye Rout between St Johns and

3. This word is written so poorly as not to be deciphered with any certainty.

4. Lake Champlain was called by the early French writers *Mer des Iroquois*, and *Lacus Irocoisionsis. — Jesuit Relations.* Winthrop, in 1666, referred to it as Lake Hiracoies. — *Winsor*, Vol. IV p. 391.

5. Richelieu River.

6. So named by Jacques Cartier, in 1535, but frequently called by early writers " The Great River," " The River of the Great Bay." In an account of his second voyage Cartier styled it *le grand fleuve de Hochelaga*, It was also sometimes called the " The River Canada." This word seems to have come from the Iroquois vocabulary, and meant " Land of the Lakes." The Indians in the vicinity of Quebec — Kebec — were called *Canadis*, by the French, or Canadacoa, in their own tongue, which became Canadian with the French, and was applied to the people of the valley of the St. Lawrence. The Indian name probably meant " People living near the water." This might mean both river and lake. The St. Lawrence was also known as the " river Saque." Quebec is the site of an Indian town known as Stadonica, and the word as accepted by the French was variously spelled as Kebec, Kebek, Quebeck, Quebec. The native word signified in that dialect " The narrowing of the water."

S[t] Francis there are two Rows of houses one on each side ye River[7] in the whole about two hundred in some places pretty thick & a fort at Chamblain as Strong as Crown Point & that the whole village of S[t] Francis Stands on an rise of Ground Mountains near fourty buildings of all Sorts that there is no fort in it but some stone houses and buildings no considerable Settlements within fifteen miles of S Francis neither did he hear of any & he apprehended there is no settlement near than Tres Riveres which is about fifteen miles from S Francis and that there is of S[t] Francis[8] & Shatacooks[9] about one hundred & Twenty fighting men that S Francis Lyes on ye north side the River of that Name & her three great Guns not mounted which they fire on Some occasion that there is young woods about the Town on ye East & north sides & that he apprehends the Distance to Mount Royal from S[t] Francis about fifty miles South-west Southerly & that M[t] Royal is Walled all Round about twelve feet high about Same thickness of Crown Point & and as is about as big as Charlestown that the Town is built Long & narrow and has many Gates to it that there are on that Island four or five hundred houses Twenty seven Cannon & two mortars all planted on a little hill within the walls and that he saw about Twenty vessels in Quebeck River at one time which were a kind of Brigantines and that during his Tarrying at S[t] Francis which was about three weeks the French carried meat at most Every day & Distributed it among the Indians and as they took no account of it nore made any Reconing about it he apprehended it Sent from the Government and also he saw five barrels of powder & some balls and Coats which the Indians told him the French gave them and that at Tres Riveres there is a Furnace where they Cast Great Guns & that fourty men were Sent from old France for that purpose. By order

JOHN CHOATE.

---

7. Richelieu River.

8. The history of St. Francis was a stormy one. It became the most noted mission in New France, as well as the strongest, until it was raided and laid in ruins by Major Rogers and his Rangers in 1759. But this expedition was not alone disastrous to the red men, who were taken completely by surprise by the whites, for many of the Rangers, as singular as it must seem, lost their way upon their return and perished in the great northern wilderness.

9. An Indian settlement below St. Francis sometimes given as Sagarac.

INDEX

This index lists all persons mentioned in the text except Mr. and Mrs. Johnson, who are prominent throughout. Citations noted as "1:" are listed in Part 1 *A Narrative of the Captivity of Mrs. Johnson.* Citations noted as "2:" are listed in Part 2 *Narrative of James Johnson.*